SHANE
WARNE
My Illustrated Career

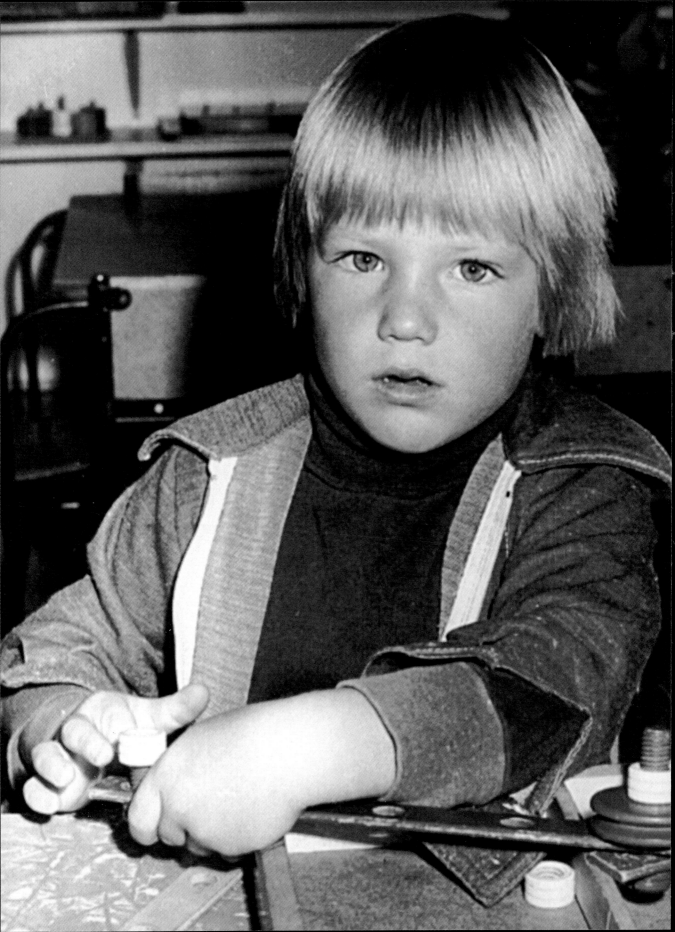

SHANE
WARNE

My Illustrated Career

CASSELL
ILLUSTRATED

CONTENTS

FOREWORD

There are very few cricketers in the history of the game who have genuinely had a great influence on the manner in which the game is played. When *Wisden* in the year 2000 came up with the splendid idea of choosing the Five Cricketers of the Century, the votes were cast by 100 selectors. The five cricketers chosen each had influenced cricket in a beneficial way.

Don Bradman received 100 votes, Garfield Sobers 90, Jack Hobbs 30, Shane Warne 27 and Vivian Richards 25.

Hobbs, Bradman and Richards were batsmen, Sobers the finest all-rounder the cricket world has seen and the careers of all four of them had graced the game over a considerable time. Warne had only been in the game for eight years, the equivalent of five minutes, and he was still playing with great success in the year 2000 when the votes were cast. What Warne had done, though, in that short time was captivate and excite the cricket world by showing there was a genuine place in the game for over-the-wrist-spin which some believed had been abandoned as a lost cause. I watched Warne's Test debut against India at the SCG in 1992. His figures were 45-7-150-1; nothing exciting there but he still looked a splendid prospect.

Although he will never be forgotten for bowling Mike Gatting at Old Trafford in 1993 with that remarkable leg-break, it was 256 days earlier that he really started his great career when he took 3 for 0 to wrap up the First Test against Sri Lanka at Colombo to give Australia a famous victory by 16 runs. He has a simple method, a few steps in from his bowling mark and then a close to flawless action to release his stock ball, the fiercely spun leg-break. He has his own mind games with the batsmen, at least once a year announcing the birth of a 'zooter,' a 'slider,' or a new-style 'flipper.' Most good batsmen are able to 'pick' what is coming out of his hand; however, playing it when it arrives at the other end is an entirely different matter. He swerves the ball in towards the pads of the right-hander, then spins it away sharply, or, it might look like the fiercely-spun leg-break but in fact slides straight on.

He is the master of his craft and his success has inspired youngsters the world over to take up the art of leg-spinning. Now we have Warne as the highest wicket-taker in the history of Test cricket and over-the-wrist spin bowling again restored to its proper place. He is the greatest I have ever seen and I have watched every leg-spin bowler since the first Sheffield Shield game I attended at the SCG on 13 January 1940, when Clarrie Grimmett took 6/118 for South Australia against New South Wales. It has been a pleasure and a privilege to watch Shane in action and I certainly hope to see him bowling in England in the Ashes battle of 2009.

RICHIE BENAUD
Coogee, Australia
March 2006

CHAPTER ONE

INTRODUCTION

I have come to believe that everybody is good at something. The problem for a lot of people is finding it. You might have a potentially great writer who never picks up a pen except to scrawl out a shopping list or an inspirational teacher who spends his working life pushing papers in an office. I was among the lucky ones. Where my ability to spin a cricket ball came from, I honestly don't know. I can only think that I was born with it. I have a skill as a cricketer and fortunately cricket found me.

When I look back over 15 years as a member of the Australian cricket team and have been very lucky to play in an era that has been very successful, I think of the way it all began and how easily I could still be drifting around from job to job, feeling unfulfilled, living off my wits and for the day. True, I played for my school teams and the local club, but as a teenager cricket was never more than a hobby. Aussie Rules was my first love, tennis probably just second and cricket was third.

Everything changed in 1989 when my beloved St Kilda decided I was not going to make the grade as an Aussie Rules player. I was too slow and not tall enough. The news struck me like a thunderbolt. With nothing to lose I decided to go to England with a mate called Rick Gough to play club cricket in Bristol. From then on cricket took over. Without planning a career I just seemed to be playing all the time. I made some progress at club level, played for Victoria and found myself walking out at Sydney on Test debut for Australia in the season of 91/92. It all happened very quickly.

A lot has happened to me since then but my proudest moment is still that day when I looked up at the electronic scoreboard and read the words: "Congratulations Shane Warne. You are the 350th Australian Test player." The scale of what I had achieved really sunk in. Test cricket had been played for more than 110 years and only 350 players had represented our great country. Put like that it felt as though I had joined a privileged group – and up to then without really trying or deserving to earn my spot.

Even then it took a while to feel at ease in those surroundings. But cricket quickly became a passion. Not everyone knows what they want at an early age; yes, we all have dreams and aspirations, but my debut was pretty lousy – we got whacked for 483 by India and my figures read 45-7-150-1. Talk about a boy among men. I soon began to contribute, though. I helped us to beat Sri Lanka with three wickets in a tight situation and then took 7 for 52 against West Indies in the Boxing Day Test of 92. And once I began my Ashes career with a ball that fizzed past Mike Gatting's grope forward and hit the stumps, things took off like never before.

I started to appreciate the history and traditions of the game, and to read about past players and to learn what everyone did. The best parts were the long chats with experienced players like Allan Border and former greats like Ian Chappell and Rod Marsh. Listening to guys like that who knew the game inside out was fascinating. Then I met Terry Jenner, a former Australia leg-spinner and a bit of a maverick himself. He has become a very dear friend and the guy I turn to if something is not quite working. I was starting to feel like a proper slow bowler, getting inside the minds of the batsmen and planning how to take wickets instead of just spinning the ball as far as I could every time!! There is a big difference in the way you go about bowling once you have a plan. Your thinking is what/when/why am I bowling a particular delivery – not waiting for the batsman to make a mistake, but out-thinking him.

> Where my ability to spin a cricket ball came from, I honestly don't know. I can only think that I was born with it. I have a skill as a cricketer and fortunately cricket found me.

Cricket has been very, very good to me, but I have had to make a lot of sacrifices along the way. Spending so much time away from home puts enormous pressure on any relationship and means I have not seen as much of my family as a father with a 'normal' job. To succeed in the game these days takes a lot of dedication. At the end of the day I think the game has cost me a hell of a lot in my personal life, along with some poor choices by yours truly. Unfortunately, you only have a short time span as a cricketer for Australia. Mine has been longer than most but,

Fast bowlers are supposed to be the aggressive ones, but I hope I have got that little bit of edge in me as well.

touch wood, it will only be around 20 percent or so of my life. You have to make the most of that opportunity but I am looking forward to spending a lot of quality time with my kids when I do retire – they are the joys of my life and my inspiration. I love them so much and can't wait to spend all my time with them, and enjoying watching them grow up and turn into young adults, and just being there for them.

Cricket is a game full of statistics and comparisons of different players and eras I believe that if you were a good player in a particular era, then you would adapt to the way the game was played in another era. Every time I pass a landmark I feel incredibly proud – 100, 200, 300 . . . all the way to 600 Test wickets. To become the leading wicket-taker of all time was beyond my wildest imagination, and makes me feel very proud. I can remember that when I started enjoying a bit of success people were coming out with all sorts of silly numbers for my eventual tally. Six hundred just seemed ridiculous, unthinkable. Records are there to be broken and I don't think you can set an upper limit. I am not big on setting targets. For one thing, what happens when you get there? It is my job to take as many wickets as I can every time I take the field.

I think I have established my place in the history of cricket, but no matter how many Tests I play and wickets I take, I like to think my biggest contribution has been to make spin bowling exciting and even fashionable, and to attract young kids to play our great game. These days captains think of spin bowling as an attacking option – except, perhaps, in England where the ambition still seems to be to keep down runs and not a great deal more. In the late 80s and early 90s the spinner only came on when a team wanted to defend. If a captain was desperate to take a wicket the spinner would be well down his list of options. My best advice when starting a spell if it's just before a break is to stay on!! You don't have to try too many things – just try to find a rhythm.

We have to remember we are part of the entertainment industry. Spectators come along to support their team but they also want to see excitement. That is why Twenty20 has been so popular in England and has started to spread to other parts of the world including Australia. I have always tried to keep people interested in the game and played every game competitively whether it is for St Kilda, Victoria, Hampshire or Australia. I have tried to become the best player I could be.

Yes, I have done a few stupid things along the way, on and off the field. There are some people who think I am a bit of an idiot and at times I would have to admit they've been right. But whether they love me or hate me, they are still interested in me and when you cut through everything else I think that is because of the way I play the game. Cricket faces a lot of competition these days, not just from other sports but from computers and the growing number of television stations. There are so many more options available for kids, and as cricketers we must never forget our responsibility to make sure our sport remains attractive. Bowling spin can be a lonely business. A lot of the time you are the only spinner in the team and on flat pitches early in a game where the ball is not turning much and the batsmen are on top it needs a lot of determination to keep going. It is not as if you can keep the batsman honest by bowling a bouncer – although I have tried on a few occasions. You just have to remember the old cliché – it only takes one ball to take a wicket. It never bothers me when a player goes down the track to hit me over the top because I know his luck will run out – eventually. I have even been known to encourage a batsman to have a go so that he gives me that chance. I would rather someone go after me rather than just block or kick the balls away. If batters go after me, I feel I have more chance of taking a wicket. It gets frustrating when they don't try to score.

Fast bowlers are supposed to be the aggressive ones, but I hope I have got that little bit of edge in me as well. I don't mind making the batsman look foolish when he plays and misses at a ball that goes past the edge. He doesn't have any sympathy for me when he whacks the ball into the stand, so why should I worry too much when the tables are turned? Off the field, of course, things are different and I've made some good friends in opposition teams. These friendships will last well into retirement, and at the end of the day, friendship, loyalty and family are the most important things in life, while taking wickets is a bit of fun.

I would split my career into three sections. What I think of as the early years came to an end around 1998. That was when I was really learning about the craft and coming to terms with

I am a wiser bowler today. That just comes with experience. The secret is to retain an air of mystery.

life as an international player. As a general rule Australia looked to bat first which meant I bowled a lot in the fourth innings of the match when conditions are best for spin.

Things changed between 1998 and the series in India in 2001 which people remember for the way India beat us after following on in Calcutta. During this period I had some quite serious injuries. Bowling leg spin puts a great strain on the body because the movements are unnatural. I suffered problems with my shoulder and spinning finger on top of the day-to-day things that crop up with playing so much. I had bowled a lot of overs in Test matches and I was still playing both forms of the game; combine this with one-day games and, well, the result was a series of operations. Little things started to creep into my action as my body compensated and although I did not like to admit it at the time I was probably less effective. I'm not at all making excuses, it is on record that I had a finger op, a shoulder reconstruction and knee cleanout. Added to this, India and some other teams were playing me better, hence the results.

Since then, and definitely since my enforced lay-off in 2003, I believe I have bowled better than ever. The last couple of years have been phenomenal, especially 2005 when I took 40 wickets in the five Ashes Tests – the best for an Australian spinner against England – and 96 in all, passing the great Dennis Lillee's record of 85 in a calendar year. By comparison, in all of 1993 I took 72 wickets in one more game. My year out, though not something I wanted, allowed time for my body to heal properly. I get a bit stiff in my back and knees when I have an intensive run of matches, but with careful management I can still be effective.

There is no doubt that Test cricket has changed in the second half of my career. Partly this is due to the increase in one-day internationals. Tactics and habits have carried into the longer game. Australia led the way – you can probably cite the introduction of Adam Gilchrist as a turning point – and other countries have followed our lead. The rate of scoring is a lot quicker now as batsmen are prepared to take more risks but, as I said earlier, the more a batsman looks to attack, the better my chance of his wicket. I may go for a few more runs these days but my strike rate is lower. This is all a positive for the great game of cricket. Look out now that Twenty20 has come into play, 400 will be on the cards.

Even if my body still allowed me to rip huge leg-breaks every ball I would not go down that route. I am a wiser bowler today. That just comes with experience. The secret is to retain an air of mystery, and be patient. If the batsman is expecting something to turn a long way then a simple, straight ball can be deadly. It all looks the same in the scorebook. So these days I make the most of variations. People raise an eyebrow when I say I am working on a new ball, but there are so many subtleties even in the simple leg-break. You can impart different degrees of spin or deliver it from different parts of the crease, wide or close to the stumps.

I can still spin the ball as much as ever, just not as consistently as ever. One ball to Marcus Trescothick at the Oval in 2005 almost went square out of the rough. I'm not sure which of us was more surprised, but he wasn't the same player for the rest of that particular innings. I generally get wickets by working on a batsman over a period of time. There was a good example at Lord's where I bowled a couple of quite big leg-breaks to Ian Bell, hoping I could set him up for an LBW or bowled with a straight one. The plan worked to perfection. And sometimes I bowl for the non-striker. Sounds odd? Well, if he has not been in form long, or not sure about facing spin, I might do something unusual to sow a seed of doubt ready for when he gets to the other end.

More than anything else I am fortunate to have played for Australia at a great time in the cricketing history of the country.

More than anything else I am fortunate to have played for Australia at a great time in the cricketing history of the country. I have played in a top class side all the way through and lots of players have become very close friends and that's what the game is about for me. I hope I don't sound big-headed by saying that I have contributed towards that success. Cricket is unusual compared to most other sports because there are so many individual statistics when really it is a team game. The most important stats are the wins and losses. I have enjoyed a lot in the first column and not too many in the second.

So when will it end? I've been asked that question on and off for roughly eight years, since my shoulder started giving me a few problems. At the time I walked off the field at the Oval with Glenn McGrath, I honestly thought I'd bowled my last ball as an Australia player in England. Had we won that game and retained the Ashes I might even have decided that was the time to bow out. Now, I'm probably less certain than ever. You can only retire once. When you've gone, that is it. The moment I feel I am holding back a young player or starting to let down my buddies is the time to call it a day.

I'm not sure if mum and dad had met when these were taken. It looks like dad might have been going through a James Dean phase with that haircut and T-shirt. He was always into his cars. Every September we would go to Queensland for a holiday and dad's target was to get there in under 20 hours. His record, scarily, was about 16. Maybe in the middle picture I'm checking the tyre before he embarks on his annual mad dash. As for mum, it isn't any surprise to see her outdoors (below left) looking so fit and healthy. She was a good runner as a child and a very keen tennis player.

Then and now … Mum and dad, Brigitte and Keith, on their wedding day in 1966 and still together 40 years on. Jason and I were lucky to have two such loving and supportive parents. They were there when we needed them but never pushed us into anything where we weren't comfortable, and when they came to watch a game of cricket or Aussie Rules they always stayed in the background. It's good to see that their sons haven't given them too many wrinkles.

Maybe it was because my parents were big on the outdoor life, but luckily I was a very healthy baby. In fact I can't remember any problems with illness as a child. What I do recall is needing stitches in my forehead when I was hit by a boomerang. I was so amazed at the way it turned around in mid-air and came back towards me that I followed its flight path and forgot to put my hand in the way.

This was taken at Apollo Bay in the early 70s. Mum grew up around here so we spent a lot of time visiting relatives and enjoying the sunshine and the sand. She was actually born in Germany but her family emigrated to Australia when she was three. I don't know if it is a trick of the light, but is this the first picture of me with a white blob of suncream on my nose?

"He was by far the smartest bowler that I played against." *MICHAEL ATHERTON, EX-ENGLAND CAPTAIN*

Here's a cute little child – butter wouldn't melt in his mouth. Looks like I might be practising the Trevor Chappell underarm delivery. Actually, my run-up looks as though it was the same back then as now. I was born in a place called Ferntree Gully but we moved house a few times while I was a kid before settling at Black Rock, a wonderful place for a kid to grow up because it was just a stone's throw from the beach.

I had to spend a whole year of my childhood using this trolley to get about. When I was eight, a boy at school jumped down on me and somehow this caused me to break both legs. At one point I was in plaster from the waist down. It wasn't a lot of fun at the time but maybe all of that wheeling around gave me the strength in my wrists and shoulders that enable me to give the ball a big rip today.

Here is an inquisitive young Shane Warne feeding a sea lion during a trip to the zoo. Being away from home so much makes it difficult to keep pets, but we do have a budgie called Yoda, named after my son Jack's favourite character from *Star Wars*. I like to think our caged bird is a bit more attractive.

Jason and I just sizing up each other across the net. I remember this court very well because it was just around the corner from home. Mum taught us both to play and we spent hours there as a family. In my mid-teens I played a lot of tennis and became quite useful, I even thought about trying to make it as a professional and stopped playing Aussie Rules and cricket for a year and reached number three in the Melbourne rankings.

I spent hours in the back garden playing cricket with my brother Jason. We would both pretend to be one of the great players of the day and imitate their mannerisms in our own little Test matches. This picture was taken at my aunt's farm in Colac, a beautiful town next to a freshwater lake about 100 miles south-west of Melbourne. Jason should have been seeing it like a football this particular afternoon given what I'm about to deliver.

My first competitive cricket was for East Sandringham Boys. I was nine at the time and I'm second from the left on the front row with my gloves and pads on – looks like I'm getting ready for a bat. In those days I wanted to bowl like Dennis Lillee, but I was also fascinated by the way some people could make the ball spin after it hit the ground. A coach called Ron Cantlon first showed me the grip for a leg-break.

Grade six, my final year at Sandringham
Primary School. I'm the boy in the black,
third from the right in the second row.
By this time sport was playing a big
part in my life. I was pretty good at PE
and I wasn't stupid when it came to the
more academic subjects but none of
them really grabbed my attention. I
went on to Hampton High and then
Mentone Boys' Grammar on a sports
scholarship.

I wince a bit when I see this picture –
and it's nothing to do with those shorts.
My problem is with the shirt. It's a
Hawthorn top, and they are one
of the rivals of St Kilda, the Aussie Rules
team I still support. Fortunately I
managed to swap the jumper. Actually
one of my favourite players was at
Hawthorn: a real rough diamond called
Dermott Brereton. He just happened to
dye his hair blond, wear an earring and
drive a Ferrari.

Members of the St Kilda Saints junior Aussie Rules team in 1987. I'm second from the right – looks as though the hairdresser had a sense of humour. I was quite handy at youth level and harboured ambitions of playing for the first team. Unfortunately my big chance for the reserves came when I was struggling with the flu. I felt I couldn't afford to turn the opportunity down but I was too weak to make an impression and the phone never rang again.

This photo (left) always makes me put my hand to my forehead and wonder if that child really is me. Sadly the answer is yes. I don't remember much about the wedding except that one of my aunts was the bride. From the expression on my face it doesn't look as though I was enjoying the occasion too much. Must have been awful having to wear a suit and bow tie at such a young age.

Good to receive a trophy instead of a few swipes of the cane from Keith Jones, headmaster at Mentone Grammar School. I lost count of the number of times I was summoned to his study. He must have had a good golf swing by the time I left judging by the amount of practice against my backside. I wasn't a bad kid, just a bit cheeky at times and I guess I could have paid more attention to my studies.

In 1985-86 I made it into the senior team at Mentone. Here, I'm on the far right of the front row. I had a reasonable amount of success in schools cricket but I wasn't what you would call a serious player. Maybe that is why I never put myself under any pressure. I was playing to enjoy myself, not to get noticed. A few of the team and some of the teachers have since said I surprised them by going as far as I have. Not as surprised as I am!

"Shane Warne is God's gift to cricket."

SACHIN TENDULKAR

A big moment when I was chosen to play for Victoria Schools against New South Wales Schools in a three-day game at Sydney. I batted at number eight, scored a half-century and then took five wickets. By that stage I had started to work on bowling although I probably still thought of myself mainly as a batsman and liked to bat in the top four at school. I guess one thing I had was the ability to give the ball a good spin.

The English summer of 1989 was one of the happiest and liveliest times of my late-teens. Spot the common denominator in these two snaps? Yes, beer played a big part in my life those few months playing club cricket in Bristol. I put on nearly 20 kilos in all and it took more than three years to get the weight back off. My excuse was the size of those pint pots in England. I still have a lot of mates in England from that time and go back to Bristol as often as I can.

Cars, karts, jet-boats – as long as they move quickly I'm happy as a kid in a sandpit. And we kicked up a bit of speed on this day off in New Zealand, surely one of the most scenic countries in the world. Steve Waugh is at the front looking completely unflustered, while I'm behind him making a bit more noise. So nothing changes there. Damien Martyn is to my left, behind the navigator.

Driving fast cars is a special passion of mine. I always like to follow the Formula One season and wouldn't have minded being a driver myself. In fact I probably go a bit too quickly on the roads at times, judging by the occasional speeding ticket dropping through the letter box. One of the perks of being a professional sportsman is the opportunity to try things like karting and feel that experience of the wind rushing past.

Working with Nike through the 90s was a great experience and privilege, not least because I met guys like Andre Agassi and, here, Michael Jordan. This picture was taken on a visit to the United States and not surprisingly I felt quite small in his presence. I think I knew more about basketball than he did about cricket but it was still fascinating to get an insight into one of the truly great sportsmen.

Sharing a drink and a smoke with the late, great Michael Hutchence, singer with the band INXS. He was a really cool customer, a wonderful guy and a good Australian who liked his cricket. He was actually a really good swimmer as a kid until he broke an arm. It was a real shock to all of the Australian team when Michael died in 1997. He left a great legacy with his songs.

D.R
PLATES

Players find different ways of relaxing
and unwinding on tour. You need to do
something to get away from cricket,
cricket, cricket and a few of the boys
have turned to music down the years.
Michael Slater, Shane Lee and bass-
playing Michael Bevan are composing
something tuneful here. Brett Lee is
another who likes to strum away on
guitar and he still plays in his band Six
And Out.

Three of the biggest influences on the early part of my career: Austin Robertson, Allan Border and John Cornell. AB was my first captain for Australia and a player I really admired as a kid. Austin, my manager, and John were two of the leading lights behind the Kerry Packer matches, which I still can't believe are not recognised as Test matches. John also worked with actor and comedian Paul Hogan.

This was a memorable week in 1997. We beat England at Old Trafford: I took nine wickets and passed Richie Benaud's record of 248 wickets for a wrist-spinner. But the highlight for me was the birth of my first baby, Brooke, on the other side of the world. I was really pumped when I saw the first pictures of her during the game and while I'd love to have been there, it was great to celebrate with my team mates.

next pages
Christmas Day makes me wish I was a kid again. It is always great to see their faces when they leave a glass of milk and some chocolate for Santa and then unwrap their presents the next morning. This is December 25th 2005 with my children and my nephew and niece. As cricketers we spend a lot of time away from home but I am lucky because the Boxing Day Test is always just a few miles away at the MCG.

29 12 2005

Like any parent I would do anything in the world for my kids. Brooke looks really smart here at home before she goes to school. Fortunately she is taking education more seriously than I did. Jack is on my shoulders (below right) – I don't think he's trying to strangle me deliberately – while something seems to have caught Summer's attention away to her left, judging by her expression (below). I look forward to spending a lot of time with them once I finish playing cricket – whenever that might be.

After a long tour or a few weeks on the road in Australia it is great to get back home, but I also enjoy holidays with the kids. Here, we have Jack in Fiji on a rare occasion when he's managed to get the Pringles away from his dad. The other two shots are in Spain, where we have spent a few weeks over the years. Summer, Jack and Brooke are getting on well together, while Jack and Summer are with me and my mum, who the kids call "Nanny Brig".

You know you're starting to get old when your kids develop the same taste in music. Here I am with Brooke at a Kylie Minogue concert. I'm not sure which of us enjoyed her more. Kylie is a great Australian. I've met her a few times and always found her good company. She is a lovely, bubbly girl from a really nice family. Dannii Minogue is another of my favourites. I often listen to one or the other in my car.

These were taken at a party in aid of Kids for Cancer, one of the charities I support through the Shane Warne Foundation. It was a great day out for Brooke, Jack and Summer and a worthwhile cause. The police helped to put on a good show and at one point they had us all handcuffed together in the back of their car. Not sure I'd like to get on the wrong side of the sergeant there with the big face.

next pages
We have found some weird and wonderful ways of travelling from place to place on tour – including helicopter. It is a great way of seeing the natural beauty of spots like this area in Sri Lanka. In other places there are lots of internal flights, not all of them especially comfortable. Personally, I enjoy going around England on the coach because you can sit back and really get to know your team mates.

previous pages
I'm not big on nostalgia, but I do remember many a happy hour at the tenpin bowling alley when I should have been at school. This shot was taken at the opening of a place called Kingpin. For the record, I want it known that I did beat Brian Lara. I think he was surprised to see the ball go straight on instead of spinning into the gutter.

I wouldn't like to place one award above another but being named BBC Overseas Sports Personality of the Year in 2005 was very special. It showed how the 2005 Ashes made such a big impression on people in England. Richie Benaud, a bloke I respect greatly as a source of cricketing knowledge, came to my club ground at St Kilda to present the prize and we fed live into the programme in London.

this page
Working out in the gym is now part and parcel of a cricketer's life. Most countries have a fitness trainer as well as a physio these days, but the key is to know what is right for the individual and not push too hard all the time. It also helps to think of the sessions as fun rather than punishment. We were laughing about something here, but Jason Gillespie still has some work to do on that bicep.

next page
I am used to having the camera pointed towards me away from the game. This time the nerdy looking man with the camcorder is not a cricket anorak but our coach John Buchanan. What there is here to catch his eye I'm not too sure – perhaps he's had an idea for the next team meeting. John's a real original who is always thinking about self-improvement. You often see him like this with his camera.

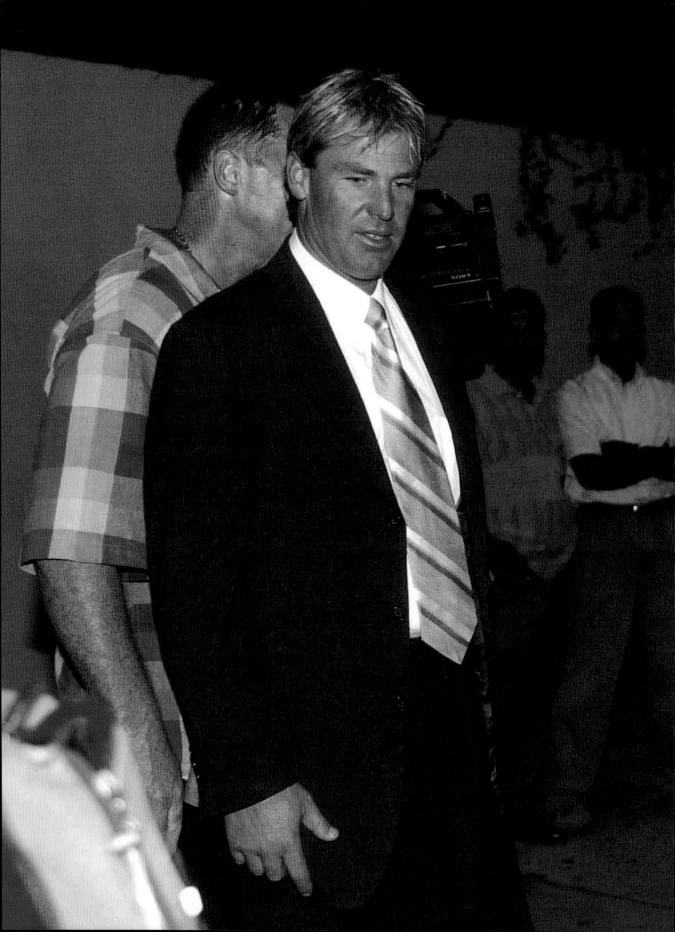

CHAPTER TWO

THE ASHES SERIES OF 2005 AND 2006/7

Unbelievable and great are overused words. But I can't think of a better way of describing the 2005 Ashes. Put it this way: if anybody had predicted the course of the series with successive nerve-jangling finishes I wonder how many people would have believed them. In 50 years' time old men and women lucky enough to be at any one of the games will have their grandchildren spellbound. I have been lucky to play in some fantastic games down the years, but never so many back-to-back that captured the public imagination in the same way, and went down to the wire.

Interest was phenomenal even before the first Test at Lord's. I wasn't too surprised because I had been in England with Hampshire the previous summer and seen how people were starting to get behind Michael Vaughan. They had a reasonably settled team and – importantly – not too many of them were scarred by previous Ashes defeats. That is why I thought the selectors were right to go with Kevin Pietersen and, to a lesser extent, Ian Bell rather than Graham Thorpe, much as I had admired Thorpe over the previous decade.

Although we were comfortable winners at Lord's I was not crowing afterwards, and certainly not predicting a 5-0 whitewash. There were some positive signs for England, especially the way that Steve Harmison set the tone in his first over. The second ball whacked Justin Langer on the elbow, and not long afterwards he struck Ricky Ponting on the head. Back in the dressing room we read this aggression as a statement of intent. The signs were there that England could knock us over if we were not at the top of our game.

In a weird way they could also take heart from the quality of our bowling. We couldn't have improved on that, and however hard you try it is impossible to be at your best every day. I had never seen Glenn McGrath bowl better in his Test career, which is really saying something.

Brett Lee bounced in with real hostility and I was pleased with my own performance after going through what I think of as a service on my action with Terry Jenner a couple of days before the game.

I wouldn't have liked to be the guy trying to condense the first day into a package of highlights. I reckon we could have bowled out England for less than 50 in their first innings, and that is after being five-down ourselves at lunch. The pre-match hype made it a tense game for the players. In fact I think people were on edge all the way through the series. That would explain the number of dropped catches. Andrew Flintoff has hands like giant spades but he spilt three or four, while Kevin Pietersen

They had a reasonably settled team and – importantly – not too many of them were scarred by previous Ashes defeats.

didn't hold one in all five games together. I like to think that I've become good and dependable in the slips but I put two or three down, including a very important one at the Oval.

To any neutral supporter the second Test at Edgbaston was a fantastic spectacle from first to last. I am not a neutral, though. I'm a proud Australia player and it does not embarrass me to say I hate losing. Sure, I take off my cap to a better side, but I'm still boiling inside. And to lose the way we did after coming so close on that Sunday morning just made this one even worse. It still amazes me to think of a two-run defeat – just one more hit to the boundary from being

I have been lucky to play in some fantastic games down the years, but never so many back-to-back that captured the public imagination in the same way.

2-0 up in the series. I don't think England would have recovered. But having said that, the way the series went: expect the unexpected.

Looking back, I think the turning point in the series is obvious. It came about three-quarters of an hour before the start at Edgbaston when McGrath tripped over a ball that had been laid out for a practice drill. I was in the middle at the time, talking to Nasser Hussain and Darren Lehmann about the pitch. When I turned round and saw McGrath on the floor I just assumed he was playing the fool as usual. I've never said this before, but I wish he was. The injury created uncertainty in our camp as we had to make a late change. For England, the sight of McGrath hobbling away and going to hospital must have given them a real lift, especially after the way he bowled at Lord's.

The other talking point was Ricky's decision to bowl first. He has taken some stick, and a lot of it is unfair in my opinion. Some weeks later an English newspaper printed a story about a bust-up in the dressing room which ended with Adam Gilchrist pulling the two of us apart. Complete nonsense! Ricky has said since that he should have batted and with the benefit of hindsight I don't think anyone would disagree. But weighing it up from his perspective, I can understand why he went the way he did. I'm a 'bat first every time' man but have had one occasion when I did the same and it will be the last.

> A spin bowler would not normally expect to bowl 25 overs on the first day. England had clearly decided to get after the bowling. They had nothing to lose.

Having dismissed England for 155 and 180 at Lord's, the option of bowling first was to get among their batsmen again straight away. There had also been a lot of heavy rain in the Birmingham area the week before. Edgbaston was less than a mile away from a tornado and witnesses said they saw rain falling onto the ground like water pouring from a tap. Ricky probably felt it better to give the seamers first use of any damp in the pitch.

I tend to belong to the Ian Chappell and the old school which says you should bat first nine times out of ten – then in that tenth case have a think and bat anyway. If batsmen have to grit out the first hour against the new ball, then that's why they are there. The pitch looked a belter to me and I knew from experience how much it could turn in the fourth innings. That is pretty much what I said to Ricky, but I think the rest of the guys wanted to bowl first. The fact is that we only lost narrowly, but a loss is a loss.

It was made to look worse by the way we used the new ball. I came on as early as the 14th over and found it tough going. A spin bowler would not normally expect to bowl 25 overs on the first day. England had clearly decided to get after the bowling. They had nothing to lose. After Lord's the attitude among the public seemed to be "same old England," so if they were going to go down they may as well have gone down fighting. And you could see the confidence of

> ## What we didn't need was a brilliant over from Flintoff which I rank as the best I have seen from anybody.

the batsmen growing as the day wore on, especially with Pietersen and Flintoff together. To score 407 in just under 80 overs was a great effort.

I could see the pitch starting to crumble towards the end of our first innings and realised we were in potential trouble with a deficit of 99. As it happened we fought back really well, but we still had to chase 282 to win. That is a big task in Test cricket, especially given the conditions, but I still thought we had a reasonable chance as long as we could get a good partnership going early. Ashley Giles was unlikely to cause problems because his job seemed to be to plug away over the wicket and try to bore us into making errors. If we were smart we could deal with that.

What we didn't need was a brilliant over from Flintoff which I rank as the best I have seen from anybody. He bowled Justin Langer, had two good shouts for lbw against Ponting and then forced an edge from our captain. When I went out to bat we were seven down with 145 still needed and England on their uppers. I remember Andrew Strauss yapping away at silly mid off, trying to prompt a mistake. I told him I would have a go when he shut up, but not until. As soon as he was quiet I slogged Giles for six. Strauss piped up again, so I started to block. I was going along quite comfortably with Michael Clarke, only for Harmison to deceive Clarke with a fantastic slower ball right at the end on the Saturday. It was a very good plan, executed perfectly.

So we were back on Sunday, still 107 short with two wickets in hand. During the warm-ups we tried to convince each other that anything could happen. Funny old game, and all that. The clichés were coming thick and fast and everyone was trying to be upbeat. Deep down, I think we all knew we were unlikely to come away with anything but defeat. Mike Kasprowicz is usually a handy guy to have at number 11 but it just happened that he was in world's worst form. The runs trickled along here and there, and the pressure grew on England. It was very tense in our dressing room and sometimes it's easier out in the middle. None of our team spoke except to

> ## Deep down, I think we all knew we were unlikely to come away with anything but defeat.

There we were, a small group of Aussies on the other side of the world giving everything to retain the Ashes. So no recriminations, just a lot of proud faces, and I felt proud of the way we fought.

cheer a run, or make a nervous joke. And then, when the greatest fightback of all time was so close, 'Kasper' tickled one down the leg side.

He was distraught afterwards. He is one of the most honest and nice guys in the game and he thought he had let down his mates. Nothing was further from the truth. He was a hero in his own way, so too Brett Lee. In those few minutes we really gelled as a team. It was pretty moving stuff. There we were, a small group of Aussies on the other side of the world giving everything to retain the Ashes. So no recriminations, just a lot of proud faces, and I felt proud of the way we fought.

Personally, this was a very, very traumatic time in my life as my marriage had hit the rocks. With Simone and the kids going home I had lost the love of my life and it seemed all I had left was my cricket. I was desperate to make sure I didn't stuff that up too. I put on a brave face in public but when my hotel room door was shut I wasn't too good. I got upset looking at photos of my kids, just wishing they were still around. Michael Clarke was a big help. I felt a bit for "Pup" as I offloaded all my troubles on to him, at a time in his life when he was trying to establish himself in the side and had his own issues. But he is my closest friend and mateship is the most important thing in life and he was there for me and I won't forget that, I really appreciated it. He spent hours with me, listening when I wanted to get something off my chest. I remember one night later in the tour when the two of us sat in the corner of a bar, both pouring our hearts out. After a few pints and a few more vodka Red Bulls I think I said that I loved him. Jeez, we were poleaxed that night. Errol Alcott, our physio, was another guy who listened a lot. Our physio, Errol Alcott, is also a bit like Dr Phil. Physios always know what is going on within a team. When you're receiving treatment there isn't much to do except talk.

The third Test at Old Trafford was another that ebbed and flowed. We suffered a setback early on when Clarke hurt his back throwing the ball back to the wicketkeeper. It is

It seemed at the time that all the 50/50 decisions and rub of the green were going England's way.

For the second time we were set up for a dramatic final day. When we arrived a couple of hours before the start, several thousand people were already waiting outside.

something that recurs with him every now and then, but we could have done without it now. As well as being a fantastic fielder he was our form batsman. It soon became clear, too, that McGrath was not going to be at his best even though he declared himself ready to return. On top of that, Jason Gillespie was struggling for confidence and Adam Gilchrist dropped a couple of catches in England's first innings, including Michael Vaughan on the way to a good hundred. It seemed at the time that all the 50/50 decisions and rub of the green were going England's way. But in truth they probably deserved that because of the way they were playing.

For the second time we were set up for a dramatic final day. When we arrived a couple of hours before the start, several thousand people were already waiting outside. Wickets fell every now and then but never in clusters, and Ricky produced one of the best innings of his life. That afternoon he gave us a taste of what was to come towards the end of the year when he established himself as the best batsman in the world. Usually a side trying to save a game in those circumstances might score a couple of hundred runs along the way, most of them very safe singles. We hit 347 and the boundaries flowed from morning to early evening. In the end we were only 52 away from actually winning.

The last four overs with Lee and McGrath at the crease were just as bad as at Edgbaston. England managed to get the ball to reverse swing through most of the series and it was hooping around in the final stages. McGrath had survived a couple of very close appeals for leg-before and he looked a prime candidate to go any minute. So before the final over Ricky sent Stuart MacGill to tell him to bat out of his crease, removing some of that risk. He took note – but forgot he needed to get back and make his ground after every ball. With the wicketkeeper standing back, Matthew Hoggard raced to the stumps so that Geraint Jones could throw him the ball. That would stop our tried and untrusted number 11 from getting off strike. At one point Hoggard had the ball in his hands over the stumps with McGrath out of his ground. Fortunately he didn't realise and threw it on instead of taking off the bails. McGrath was oblivious to all this. He walked into the dressing room expecting a hero's reception, only to be described as something a bit stronger than an idiot.

In his own (thankfully) inimitable way he'd done his bit and the bottom line was that we were still level at 1-1. Sometimes in those circumstances the draw can seem like a win. We did not exactly celebrate, but we were happy as well as relieved. This was the night I first witnessed Freddie Flintoff's ability to take off a bottle top with his teeth. Some of the England team had come into our dressing room with the beer and we couldn't find an opener. Fred just said "Give it here", opened his mouth and went "crunch". The teams spent several hours together that night talking about cricket and life in general. There was a lot of respect between us, and to me the spirit in which the whole series was played was a lesson to everyone about how the game should be played.

> When some of the spectators behind me started singing, "We wish you were English", I felt I had finally won them over.

Meanwhile, my body was starting to feel the pain. At various times I had problems with my shoulder, back, abductor and knees. Part of this was general wear and tear which I supposed I had to expect as a 35-year-old going on 36. It was heightened by bowling a lot of overs in back-to-back matches and getting hit so many times by hostile bowling. I never felt like getting out against the short ball – I was more concerned with the swinging yorkers – but that doesn't mean I enjoyed getting bruised in the chest. At one point I wondered if I might have to miss the Trent Bridge Test. In the build-up I needed three or four sessions each day in the pool and another two or three in the treatment room. I would be going out as Glenn McGrath came in; we should have fitted revolving doors.

Once I got into my bowling rhythm I didn't feel too bad. And the adrenalin pumping through my body would have helped. In any normal series this match would have been considered a thriller. By now I think the crowds expected nothing less. We were still feeling pretty confident as a team because although England had the better of things at Old Trafford they needed to win the series to reclaim the Ashes whereas a draw was good enough for us. That is why I thought and said that the pressure was on the home side, but a few critics thought I was trying to play mind games with the opposition. All I did was state a fact. There must be some easy money in psychology if that's all there is to it.

As it worked out we did not play consistently enough through the game, but then England didn't let us. The Trent Bridge Test match we thought we were about 50-odd runs short, and as it turned out we were not far away again but England deserved their win. And so it boiled down to the final Test at the Oval, and in the days ahead the weather forecasters seemed to be working overtime. We were desperate, for obvious reasons, to be able to have five clear days. Unfortunately, a poor prediction for the weekend proved accurate and we ran out of time. Nobody will know whether we would have scored the 342 we needed to win. Given the way the series unfolded, the smart money would have been on a tie.

I thought that if we could build a big first innings score we would have a really good chance because, as at Edgbaston, I expected the ball to turn big time later on. As it was, I managed to take five wickets even on the first day – though I was shattered again afterwards – and with Justin Langer and Matthew Hayden both scoring hundreds, we put ourselves in a great position. They were criticised for taking an offer of bad light and in the end we did lose a longer time than they would have imagined in a game where we really needed every minute. These things are always difficult and you have to back the judgement of the batsmen out in the middle. When you go off, the delay could be a minute or an hour.

Flintoff had another sensational game. This time he bowled unchanged through 14.2 overs on the fourth day, broken only by lunch. By rights he should have been tired by the time I came out to bat. No chance. He was quick, nasty and moved the ball a long way. This was his first five-for against us and, with a hundred at Trent Bridge and other contributions over the weeks, he was a clear candidate for England's man of the series. You could see their team thinking that while Freddie was on their side with the ball in his hand, everything would be fine. Usually it was.

Going in to the final day we had a maximum of 98 overs to take nine England wickets and knock off whatever that left us by way of a target. There was no need to panic but at the same time we could not afford too many mistakes. Unfortunately I made one

> You could see their team thinking that while Freddie was on their side with the ball in his hand, everything would be fine. Usually it was.

> There was a lot of respect between us, and to me the spirit in which the whole series was played was a lesson to everyone about how the game should be played.

of the most costly. I gave everything in the series, took 40 wickets and scored 249 runs, so I am not going to blow up the Kevin Pietersen drop. How did it happen? Well, I was surprised at the lack of pace off the bat when he pushed at Brett Lee. It came face-high at slip and I think I took it too early. Ninety-nine times out of a hundred I would have held it and said it was a regulation chance. In these situations you have to get on with the game, keep encouraging the bowlers and the fielders and hope the wicket falls quickly.

> I think 2-2 would have been the fairest result, but if there had to be a winner, then it could only be England. Except at Lord's, they didn't allow us to play as well as we wanted.

There was no guarantee we would have won if I'd caught it. We were still in a strong position in mid-afternoon. What did for us was a stand of 109 between Pietersen and Ashley Giles. It lasted 26 overs so by the time Glenn McGrath knocked out Pietersen's off stump the game was over. The crowd sensed it and as the afternoon wore on I began to think I was a gatecrasher at somebody else's party. When some of the spectators behind me started singing, "We wish you were English", I felt I had finally won them over. I appreciated that. Crowds are entitled to shout for their own team, but for the most part they were generous towards us and appreciated good cricket.

I think 2-2 would have been the fairest result, but if there had to be a winner, then it could only be England. Except at Lord's, they didn't allow us to play as well as we wanted. We were a pretty good Australia team, not the best ever but a long way from being the worst. However, for the first time since my Ashes debut in 1993, England had a group of potential match-winners instead of just one or two. Andrew Flintoff is the obvious one, but Steve Harmison, Michael Vaughan, Kevin Pietersen and Simon Jones have all become good cricketers and they have honest, reliable players around them as strong back-up; together they make up an excellent cricket side.

They also had depth in the bowling attack. In the past we knew that if we could get through a spell from Andy Caddick or Darren Gough we could bank on a four-ball an over because their first and second change were not of the same quality. This time we did not get any respite. They covered all bases with orthodox swing, reverse, seam and steepling bounce. And their attitude was spot on. They were not in awe of us. They worked out some good plans and carried them out. It is as if they said: "We're sick of losing to you and it won't happen again."

I am not sure we did a lot wrong. Players can feel in great touch in practice and just cop a few good balls in the big matches. But I would say that behind the scenes we had a lot of team meetings which I'm not sure were always very productive. I'm not saying that's the reason, but it was just talking around in circles rather than getting out and doing something. I believe that cricket is best kept simple. You have plans for players but if you over-analyse and talk for too long you can go around in circles and finish even more confused than when you start. If a batsman is having a lot of trouble with spin or short balls, for example, then make sure you get your spinner or fast bowler on straight away, or you end up just saying, "Bowl a good channel," "Be patient," and so on. In other cases you can end up with a Plan A, Plan B, Plan C all the way to Plan Z.

Without having a pop at John Buchanan, it is fair to say that he isn't a classic coach. His style suits some players better than others, like all coaches. I remember at his first team meeting he said that he was there to improve us as people first and cricketers second, but I am not sure the responsibility of a coach stretches as far as life skills. You can talk all you like and hatch as many plans as your brain can handle but out there on the field you have to adapt and adjust, and sometimes you need Plan A, B, C, and Z. In the real world opponents will not always fall into the traps that sounded perfect the night before. I believe that being a Test cricketer comes down to self-belief, a simple, sound technique, an instinct for the game, plenty of ticker and, above all. the right attitude. A computer isn't much use when Freddie Flintoff is reverse swinging the ball into your feet at 90 miles per hour.

> We took a lot of criticism back in Australia. People back home were not used to losing to England. At least the cricket had captured the imagination of the public.

We took a lot of criticism back in Australia. People back home were not used to losing to England. At least the cricket had captured the imagination of the public. I remember turning out for a grade match with St Kilda and seeing a crowd of more than a thousand. We needed to fight back strongly to make the public believe we were still a good side. By winning the ICC Super Series and then beating West Indies and South Africa we did all we could to convince them. And I can say this with absolute certainty: England are going to have to be at their very best again to retain the Ashes on our home soil.

If the last series was spectacular then this one could be even better. My guess is that the key players will be the same as last time. In fact I wouldn't be surprised if England stick with the XI who played from Lord's through to Trent Bridge before Simon Jones picked up an injury. On our side you can look at the usual suspects. If Matty Hayden, Ricky Ponting, Adam Gilchrist, Glenn McGrath and myself are all close to top form I think we have a great chance. For England, you have to look at the pace bowlers again. Among the batsmen, Michael Vaughan played beautifully out here in 2002/03 and Kevin Pietersen has shown signs of being special. Then there is Flintoff, of course.

A computer isn't much use when Freddie Flintoff is reverse swinging the ball into your feet at 90 miles per hour.

In 2005 England won a lot of the big moments. Flintoff is so important because he can change games with bat or ball. He showed that he has great stamina as well as strength. It will be interesting to see how he copes on the harder, bouncier pitches. Pietersen can be an even more dangerous batsman because he is slightly unorthodox and hits the ball into areas you don't expect. If he looks as though he ought to be vulnerable then nobody has yet found him out. He has a good temperament and whatever happens against us I think he has a great future as long as he doesn't get carried away with off-field stuff and keeps his feet on the ground.

We need to get at their middle order early because Marcus Trescothick and Andrew Strauss gave them some pretty good starts last time. Trescothick has a certain way of playing that works for him most of the time and he can set a good tempo for the innings. He struggled a little bit in Australia in 2002/03 but seems to have learned from the experience. As I said earlier, it comes down to knowing your own game and not always worrying about every dot and comma in the manual, and knowing yourself.

Where England could get caught out is their lack of spin bowling options. The pitches will definitely turn at Sydney and Adelaide. Brisbane I rate as the best track in the world. It does give some help to the seam bowlers early on, which is why I have some sympathy for Nasser

We need to get at their middle order early because Marcus Trescothick and Andrew Strauss gave them some pretty good starts last time.

Hussain when he decided to put us in on the last tour. I know that decision may haunt England captains but it could be that bowling first is the best option again, even though spinners are sure to come in to play on days four and five. That one might be a good toss to lose.

There will come a time when Ashley Giles has to do something more than keep an end tight for the pace bowlers. There was a lot of talk in 2005 about England players knowing their roles but I think Ashley, quietly, will be disappointed with his figures, especially as he had the benefit of bowling on the fifth day at Old Trafford and other Tests. Shaun Udal may be a good option as an off-spinner because he gets bounce, which is very handy on Australian pitches. England really need to unearth a slow bowler in his 20s who can develop into a wicket-taking threat. At the moment it is a big weakness in their attack.

For a few of us this is likely to be our last Ashes series. I have no doubt this will become an issue in the build-up and we will have to deal with those questions. I think it will just add to our motivation. Losing an Ashes series is bad enough, but when you don't have a chance to rectify it the hurt must be even worse. Since 2005, of the older guys, Hayden has knocked off hundred after hundred, Gilchrist has found some form again and I am coming off the most successful year of my life; as for Ricky he has dominated and become the best in the world.

The selectors have made a few changes and Mike Hussey for one has strengthened the middle order. He has a very good reputation in England through county cricket, and rightly so. He is one of those guys who just loves batting. In any other side he would be an established Test player by now. His nickname of "Mr Cricket" is spot on. And I think Michael Clarke is too good a strokemaker to be out for too long. There seems to be a policy now to have an all-rounder at six or seven, so Shane Watson will probably fit in at some point, challenged by Andrew Symonds.

Of the specialist bowlers, my guess is that Shaun Tait, who made his debut at Trent Bridge, will be fit again and back hovering around the squad. Even in that one

> For a few of us this is likely to be our last Ashes series. I have no doubt this will become an issue in the build-up and we will have to deal with those questions.

> My guess is that the key players will be the same as last time.

game he produced some swinging balls at a good enough pace to trouble batsmen. I'm not sure he was quite clear about his role in England, but that will come with experience. If he stays fit he could be our new ball bowler for a few years.

As to a suggestion from left-field, I want to throw in the name of a guy who may not be known in England but who did well in the last Australian season – Shane Harwood. I know him pretty well from Victoria. He is a fast bowler in his early 30s who offers something different. At around 5ft 11in he skids the ball on to batsmen and makes them hurry with their shots. He is a late developer – very late in cricket terms – but Ashes history is littered with unlikely guys who come from nowhere to seize the moment. Shane Harwood: you read it here first.

And I can say this with absolute certainty: England are going to have to be at their very best again to retain the Ashes on our home soil.

After an incredible first day at Lord's where everything seemed to happen quickly the game settled and we managed to get our noses further and further in front. A target of 420 was always going to be too much for England. I was looking forward to bowling at Ian Bell because he was making his first appearance against us and I wanted to lay down a marker. In the second innings I set him up for a classic lbw – a few leg breaks followed by one that went straight on.

I started the season playing with Kevin Pietersen at Hampshire and we exchanged plenty of friendly banter all the way through the series. His world took off over the weeks, probably a bit like mine in 1993. He was one of the positives for England in defeat at Lord's with two half-centuries on debut. Even though England were struggling he stuck to his natural, attacking game – a taste of things to come at the Oval.

Lord's is a great place to celebrate either on the balcony with the team and the back-up staff or with a quiet drink inside. The only disappointment from a personal point of view was not quite making it onto the honours board. It takes five wickets in an innings for that. I had four to my name in the second innings only for Glenn McGrath to remove Simon Jones – with me taking the catch at slip. That was the third time I had taken four wickets in a Test innings at the ground.

Not sure I'd like to face that mean-looking guy from 22 yards. The painting was commissioned by the MCC to hang in the Long Room at Lord's. Here I am with the artist, a lovely girl called Fanny Rush. At the unveiling somebody said she had been told to paint out my package as it was too big!! I thought it was a joke but it was reported as fact. I'm still not sure about that. Only two other Australians, Sir Donald Bradman and Keith Miller, are up there, so this was a very big honour.

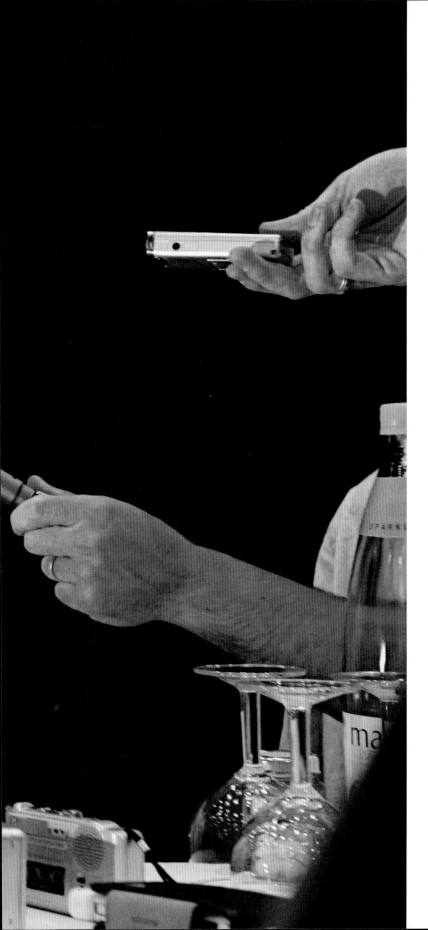

previous pages
Australia used to start every Ashes
tour at Worcester, one of the prettiest
grounds in England. This time we
played there midway through the
series, by which time Glenn McGrath
and I were both in need of some rest
and recovery. In this picture it looks as
though the bloke we call Pigeon
(because of the shape of his legs) is
thinking of taking up leg-spin while
I'm checking his grip for the off-cutter.
Maybe we're best sticking to what
we know.

Looking a bit pensive as a press
conference gets under way – not sure
what I'd done wrong this time! Dealing
with the media is part and parcel of
sport. I've been lucky in that most
things written about me have been
very nice. There are times when it has
become intrusive but cricket needs
the media. Sometimes I get accused of
playing mind games through the
newspapers. I just try to be as honest
as I can and say what I think.

I wanted to make a statement when I came on to bowl in the second innings at Edgbaston. It was coming towards close on the Friday and if I could do something special it would give their batsmen something to think about overnight. This ball was one of the best I have ever bowled. Andrew Strauss tried to pad up but it turned across him and hit leg stump. You can get an idea of how much it spun by looking at the position of his front leg. I christened Strauss "the new Daryll" after my biggest rabbit, Daryll Cullinan. In fairness, he worked hard and scored two hundreds later on.

I think it was on the previous Ashes tour in 2001 that our bowlers began a trend of raising an arm with ball in hand after taking five wickets in an innings. We see it as the equivalent of a batsman holding up his bat when he completes a hundred. So here I am at Edgbaston (below left) after taking the wicket of Steve Harmison on the third day. I finished with 6 for 46 but the last wicket pair, Andrew Flintoff and Simon Jones, put on 51 crucial runs to set up a great finish.

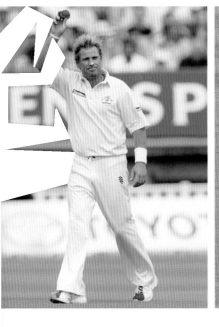

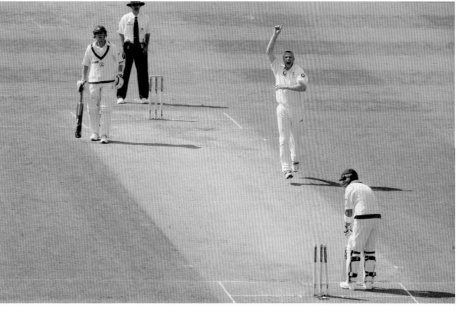

Going into that final Sunday at Edgbaston I don't think even we believed we could win. But the runs came down and Brett Lee and I started to work in tens – 90 needed, then 80 and so on. We got to within 53 and were going nicely when I was freakishly out hit wicket. To protect myself from the yorker from Flintoff I decided to go across my stumps. Unfortunately I went too far over and back, lost my balance and could feel my right foot making a slight but fatal connection against off stump. The celebrations around me were enough to confirm that I'd dislodged a bail.

Wickets come in bizarre fashion and the 600th of my Test career was one of the strangest. Marcus Trescothick went for the sweep but the ball somehow came off the back of his bat and Adam Gilchrist held a catch via his knee, chin and whatever else happened to get in the way. I remember Michael Vaughan coming over to shake my hand which was a nice touch and typical of the good sportsmanship through the series.

I was having a tough time around this period as Simone and the kids had gone back to Australia. Before they left, my elder daughter Brooke gave me a white wristband bearing the word STRENGTH. She said: "Daddy, you've got to be strong." I thought that was a pretty good effort for an eight-year-old, so when I took my 600th wicket I kissed the band and said: "Brookey, that's for you." I don't usually get emotional on the cricket field but I struggled to hold back the tears this time.

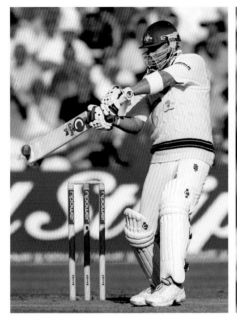

All through the summer I felt I was batting pretty well. I'd scored my maiden first-class hundred for Hampshire and was on 78 not out at the close on Saturday. I soon went to 86 next morning when Simon Jones came on. His first ball was short, so I cut it away. I remember thinking 'just keep bowling it there buddy'. The next one was almost in the same place and I creamed it again – only to see it head straight to Ashley Giles on the boundary. So near but so far.

After Edgbaston, the Old Trafford Test produced another amazing finish. Basically we had to bat out the final day to survive. We showed a lot of courage to do so with many a close shave along the way. It looks like Andrew Flintoff almost got me here – just shows that not everything went for him. With England attacking all day there were plenty of gaps in the field and at one point I thought of asking Ricky Ponting whether it was worth having a dart. Don't think he would have been too impressed.

Even though England needed just 129 to win the fourth Test there were still some twists and turns along the way. They had spent nine hours in the field so they were bound to be tired. I felt we were 50 or so runs short, but the way wickets started to fall another 20 could have been enough. Their seventh wicket fell on 116 and I didn't think Steve Harmison and Simon Jones would last long if we could get them in. But we couldn't quite make that breakthrough and Matthew Hoggard was celebrating here after Ashley Giles clipped me for the winning runs

The Trent Bridge crowd gave me a generous reception for those four second innings wickets but it wasn't too long before they broke into a chorus of "Ashes coming home". It seemed as though the whole of England was joining in. The dressing rooms at the ground are on split levels, one on top of the other, and the noise of the England boys celebrating could be heard through our ceiling. In little more than a month the series had turned.

This is not meant to sound like sour grapes, but I don't think umpires Aleem Dar and Steve Bucknor had their best ever games at Trent Bridge. Umpiring is a really difficult job and it is harder now than ever because television has so many cameras and tools to scrutinise decisions. It isn't a job I would ever consider. I thought I had two good shouts for lbw against Flintoff in the first innings and Simon Katich was unlucky when we followed on. Overall, though, England did not let us play as well as we wanted.

Going to the Oval was a new experience for me this time. In the past we had always retained the Ashes before the final game. I knew the senior players had to set an example to level the series. Unfortunately we lost the toss because I would have fancied my chances on a five-day pitch. Once again it meant bowling a lot of overs on the first day, but I did have some success with Simon Katich producing a brilliant catch to remove Andrew Strauss and Kevin Pietersen playing on. I bowled 76 overs in the game overall but with 12 wickets I could again hold the ball aloft.

next pages
One last push – that was our attitude going into the final day. Glenn McGrath bowled a good spell early on and when I took this return catch to get rid of Andrew Flintoff before lunch we were in a strong position. Fred is one of those players who sometimes takes a few overs to get his feet moving and feel loose. If you can get the ball in the right place early on he gives you a chance. With my creaking body this was a decent take at about ankle height.

You have to hand it to Kevin Pietersen.
He loves the limelight and I suppose
the final day of the Ashes was exactly
his stage. What his 158 showed was the
importance of playing your natural
game. Before lunch he seemed a bit on
edge so that when I dropped him we
probably thought another chance
would come along. But after lunch he
was a different player. It takes some
bottle to keep hooking Brett Lee with
two men back knowing how much is
at stake. A classic case of fortune
favouring the brave.

These two pictures cannot have been taken more than a couple of seconds apart but they capture the bitter-sweet feeling as Glenn McGrath and I walked off at the Oval for the last time together in a Test match in England. The applause and the standing ovation were very moving. On the other hand we had lost the Ashes after 16 years. It just felt right to walk off together like this. I don't know about my old buddy, but I felt shattered in every sense.

next pages
Some of the presentation ceremonies feel like they go on forever. I think the sponsors were keen to milk this one for as long as they could. I had just received a medal and some champagne as our player of the series and I am rejoining some very thoughtful-looking team mates. People wondered how we would take defeat after so long. I think we were very dignified. We could not hide the fact that we were beaten by a better side.

CHAPTER THREE

THE ASHES

I have played in seven Ashes series and been on the winning side in six of them. That has been a fair reflection of the sides. England went through the 90s without ever getting it together against us while Australia were always very strong. I would not like to say the 1993 team was better than 1997 or 2001. All three were fantastic. Even in 2005 I never went into a game against England feeling part of the weaker side.

Touring has changed considerably since my first series in 1993. That summer we played 15 first-class matches as well as the Tests, and three one-day internationals. There was a lot more beer consumed, more socialising and many hours spent listening to the senior guys. We had official functions but nowhere near as many commitments for sponsors. And the families are around these days – in 1993 wives were not allowed to stay in the team hotel. Thinking back, it seems like a different age – everything has changed. Training used to be a lot shorter but more competitive in the nets; now there is far too much cricket played.

> I would not like to say the 1993 team was better than 1997 or 2001. All three were fantastic.

As far as cricket goes, you could say the same about one England side as any other, at least until 2005. They always seemed to be intimidated. Whatever they said in the papers – and even some of that was very cautious – they never looked as though they really thought they might beat us. I would guess that we won 90 percent of the key moments in the Tests. England might drop a catch, collapse after a good partnership or relax the pressure after a tight period with the ball. The side never seemed to be settled and they had so many injury problems. I wonder how much some of them really wanted to take us on.

On my first tour we had a very strong batting side. Mark Taylor and Michael Slater were a great combination at the top, then came David Boon, Allan Border and the Waugh boys. The plan was to bat first, pile up a mountain of runs in the first two days and give ourselves a chance to bowl sides out twice. We never thought about run rates. Scoring 300 in a day was almost unheard of, but we did make some big, big totals. Guys like Boon and Border were hewn from the old school. They knew what it was like to lose to England in the mid-80s and were determined not to let it happen again.

Australia have been blessed with tremendous batsmen all through my time. I think that comes from learning to play on quick and reliable pitches back home. Matty Hayden flourished, eventually to become one of Australia's great openers and Ricky Ponting, an incredible talent as a youngster, now deserves to rank as one of our best-ever number threes. Then there are guys like Damien Martyn, Justin Langer and, of course, Adam Gilchrist, who has changed the whole way selectors think about their wicketkeepers.

Among the best performances by England players, I can think of Darren Gough's hat-trick in Sydney and, although I think he only took three wickets, a very good spell by Andy Caddick at Trent Bridge in 2001. But it wasn't until 2005 that England really put an attack together that could bowl in partnerships and keep both ends tight for longer than a few overs. Gough and Caddick could be a handful with the new ball but there must be a long list of bowlers who played once or twice against us and then disappeared. Caddick could have been one of the best in the world, but you always felt that if you got on top of him early then you were OK.

I have generally enjoyed myself against England. Their batsmen do not get much practice against wrist spin so even experienced players like Stewart and Atherton could struggle.

But it wasn't until 2005 that England really put an attack together that could bowl in partnerships and keep both ends tight for longer than a few overs.

> **I will never forget the Gatting ball at Old Trafford – I won't be allowed to even if I wanted.**

On the batting side, there was a good hundred by Graham Thorpe in Perth in 1994/95, Mark Butcher's unbeaten match-winning century at Headingley in 2001 and a double-hundred by Nasser Hussain at Edgbaston in 1997. But I think Graham Gooch's batting in 93 was amazing – he was the hardest English batsman that I bowled to. And Michael Atherton was one I thought was always trying to read your game plan, and work out what you were up to. That was my second Ashes tour and we were in a bit of trouble after losing the one-day series and then going one-down in the Tests. But England couldn't keep it up. Glenn McGrath bowled brilliantly to take eight wickets at Lord's and although the game was rained off the initiative had swung our way.

McGrath bowled even better at Lord's in 2005, but there are so many outstanding performances by Australians it is hard to know what to leave out. My first choice has to be Merv Hughes all the way through that 1993 series. Bone was rubbing against bone in his knee and when he hobbled back to fine leg at the end of an over, you'd think his career was over. Then five minutes later he would steam in again. One of my clearest memories is of Merv slumped in the dressing room at the Oval with ice packs on every joint you could imagine. He inspired youngsters like myself by playing on through all that pain. Merv was an under-rated bowler and has a better cricket brain than people might think. It is just well hidden behind that big moustache.

Of our batsmen I think of Border's double-hundred at Headingley in 1993 and Steve Waugh's two hundreds at Old Trafford in 1997. Mark Taylor had won the toss and decided to bat despite

> **I called him Mr Gooch and he wasn't sure whether I was being cheeky; I wasn't – it was total respect.**

ideal conditions for seam and swing bowling. He worked out that if we gritted things out to start with we could put England under pressure later on. It was a brave decision but Waugh stood up to everything, never flinched and just got on with the business of scoring runs. Sometimes you forget about elegance and just look at the scoreboard.

I will never forget the Gatting ball at Old Trafford – I won't be allowed to even if I wanted. Then there was David Boon, a guy we called the "keg on legs", producing an incredible catch to complete my hat-trick at Melbourne in the 1994 Boxing Day Test, and Michael Slater cutting the first ball of the 2002-03 series to the boundary at Brisbane after Nasser had put us in.

The strangest dismissal would be when Graham Gooch handled the ball in my first match at Old Trafford. Actually, bowling to Gooch was a big privilege because he was one of the England players I did admire, and was the best England player I have played against. I called him Mr Gooch and he wasn't sure whether I was being cheeky; I wasn't – it was total respect. And the funniest moment? It has to be Ian Healy, again at Old Trafford, when he reached a hundred and wanted to celebrate but couldn't undo the chin strap on his helmet. Talk about missing the moment.

I have generally enjoyed myself against England. Their batsmen do not get much practice against wrist spin so even experienced players like Stewart and Atherton could struggle – that's if Atherton made it beyond McGrath in the first place. And some of our celebrations have been highlights in themselves. At the Oval in 2001 we burnt a bail to create our own Ashes – only to let off one of the smoke alarms.

The expression on Mike Gatting's face says it all. This was my first ball in an Ashes Test and I reckon I still get asked about it more than anything else. It has been described as "the ball from hell" and "the ball of the century". To be honest I would have been happy with one that hit the right spot and didn't go for runs. But I knew it might be more than that by the way it curved in to the batsman in the flight – this is usually a sign it will turn. Even then it was a fluke to spin as much as it did. I might even have apologised to Gatting as he walked off.

After the Gatting ball it seemed I couldn't do anything wrong in that Test match. I finished with eight wickets and if I think of games that really changed my life then Old Trafford 1993 would have to be right up there. This picture was taken after I bowled Robin Smith in the second innings. He became one of my great mates in the game and I reckon the delivery that got him in the first innings was even better than the one people remember.

next pages
A hat-trick against England is bound to be something to cherish but this was extra special because it happened at my home ground, the MCG, during the 1994-95 series. I'd removed Phil DeFreitas and Darren Gough and I remember Alec Stewart at the non-striker's end turning to me and saying: "You won't get a better chance than this." Damien Fleming had taken a hat-trick in Pakistan a few months earlier and his advice was to bowl my stock ball because that was my best. Devon went forward, got hit on the gloves and David Boon took a great catch to his right at short leg.

Winning the fifth Test at Trent Bridge meant we retained the Ashes again in 1997. This was another of my best balls, a dipping leg-spinner that turned a long way out of the footmarks to bowl Nasser Hussain. Mark Waugh and Greg Blewett are rushing over to offer congratulations. This was in the days before Nasser became England captain. He was a strong-minded guy and so intense that I'm not sure all of his team felt at ease playing under him.

I got a bit of a rap from some journalists for this victory wiggle on the balcony at Trent Bridge. The picture doesn't show that I was moving to the song of the crowd, and there weren't any complaints from my team mates. If a bloke can't celebrate retaining the Ashes, then when can he let his hair down? We went on to lose the final match at the Oval but we were the better side by a fair way overall.

The final Test of the 1998-99 series at Sydney was my comeback after a major shoulder operation. Stuart MacGill, left, had done a good job while I was away and the selectors picked us both for this game. He took 12 wickets here while I picked up a couple easing my way back. Stuey is a good, aggressive spin bowler who gives it a real tweak both ways. I enjoy bowling in tandem and overall we've done well together, but the selectors do not always want two leggies in the same side.

Having established a run of Ashes wins against England we always felt it important to make a good start to a series to try to re-open those old wounds. Part of bowling spin in particular is to try to get into the heads of the batsman, to make them think there is something magical they don't understand. So this was a great way for me to begin the 2001 campaign – second ball, Mark Butcher caught by Ricky Ponting.

My 400th Test wicket came towards the end of a very long day at the Oval: Alec Stewart caught by Adam Gilchrist trying to steer towards third man. The second new ball was only six overs old and he might have been undone with some extra bounce. Number 399 had come five hours earlier but fortunately I didn't have to wait as long to pin victim 401 – Andy Caddick went first ball. I couldn't help a little bow to the crowd.

Glenn McGrath and I were level on 31 wickets for the 2001 series when Phil Tufnell walked to the crease as England's last man. He wasn't going to last long but I hoped he might be able to at least see out the over so I could get a crack from the other end. Instead he lasted two balls, pushing at the second to give me a catch at slip. At least I can claim a half-share in the wicket.

next pages
This scene has been quite familiar in my time as an Australia player – lining up for the camera at the end of a successful Ashes series. Here I am with Adam Gilchrist and Steve Waugh at the Oval after winning 4-1 in 2001. England had all sorts of injuries and never got going. We would have completed a 5-0 whitewash except for the fact that Mark Butcher played the innings of his life at Headingley, but victory overall was in the bag by that stage.

Here's a scene Nasser Hussain must have replayed over and over again in his mind – the first toss of the 2002-03 series in Brisbane. He decided to bowl and with Simon Jones suffering a horrific injury was helpless as we finished the day on 364 for 2. In fairness to Nasser, Brisbane is a very difficult pitch to judge and his bowlers didn't do as well as he would have expected. Similarities, then, with Ricky Ponting's decision to bowl at Edgbaston nearly three years later.

Celebrating the wicket of Alec Stewart in Brisbane – I've managed to dismiss him 14 times in Test matches, more than any other batsman. The Test finished as badly for England as it had begun, with us bowling them out for 79. They really struggled in this series from the moment they landed with Darren Gough and Andrew Flintoff unfit. It was only in Sydney when they won a game – Glenn McGrath and myself were both injured.

CHAPTER FOUR

ASIA

When I think of breakthrough series for Australia, two come to mind. The first was in 1995 when we beat West Indies. Once we succeeded in the Caribbean we could call ourselves the top side in the world. The second came nine years later when we finally beat India on their home soil and answered the sole remaining question that hung over us. We had now overcome all opposition home and away and could take our place alongside the great West Indies and Australia teams of the past.

My own record in India is rubbish, and there are a few reasons for this: during the period between 1998 and 2001 I underwent five operations and was not very successful against anyone, but, having said that, the Indians played me the best out of anyone in my time. I took 14 wickets in three Tests in 2004, and it was annoying to miss out on the fourth when I broke my thumb in the nets. The ball turned square those two days in Mumbai as Michael Clarke took 6 for 9 with his slow left arm and Harbhajan Singh twice opened India's bowling. I proved to myself that if I was fit I could do well against the Indians.

> On my first trip to India I asked whether we could have a few tins of baked beans shipped over and the press billed it as an SOS call.

It did not really matter because we were already 2-0 up following wins in Bangalore, where Clarke scored a brilliant hundred on debut, and in Nagpur, where Jason Gillespie took nine wickets. On a personal level I had shown that I could be a threat in India. Three years earlier we went into the series on the back of 15 straight Test wins, made it 16 straight away in Mumbai but were undone by incredible batting and Harbhajan's spin in

Calcutta and Chennai. Everybody remembers Calcutta for VVS Laxman's double hundred and partnership with Rahul Dravid. We chose to enforce the follow-on which is the only way they could have won.

This time our preparation was perhaps a bit more thorough and their batsmen never had the same impact. It helped us that Sachin Tendulkar missed the start of the series because of tennis elbow. Not surprisingly he was some way from his best when he did return, and neither Dravid nor Laxman caused anywhere near as many problems. I have dismissed Dravid eight times in all, more than any other bowler in Tests. He is a class act and to bowl him and get him a few times is very satisfying.

Touring India is an amazing and interesting experience. You could read all the guide books (which I haven't) and spend hours listening to travellers but still be dumbstruck in your first few hours in Mumbai or Calcutta. There are things to make you laugh, others that bring you to tears and some that have you shaking your head in disbelief. People are everywhere. The noise is incessant and the rich smell can knock you backwards. It brings out the strongest emotions but unless you remain patient, level-headed and accept the odd stomach complaint as an occupational hazard, you are beaten. It does take a tour or two to feel comfortable and understand the conditions.

Some of the old players turn white when they recount their horror stories from the sub-continent. These days, we have no excuses. The hotels are almost always of a good international standard. Fortunately for me, I can get the food I like. I am not big on curries or spices. There is not much I can eat. Anything with cheese is good, pizza is a staple and I love a big bowl of nachos with dips. Vegetables are a problem. On my first trip to India I asked whether we could have a few tins of baked beans shipped over and the press billed it as an SOS call. I hope I'm not that bad. People were not getting too close after the shipment arrived.

I cannot imagine India ever having problems producing players, although an interesting period lies ahead with Tendulkar, Dravid and Laxman all in their 30s. Just as the 60s and 70s were a golden period for their spinners, so the past decade will be remembered for their batsmen. Because the crowds always expect so much, young players may feel daunted

Players can be worshipped – the story about Tendulkar wearing a false beard to go to the cinema is true.

coming into the side. Players can be worshipped – the story about Tendulkar wearing a false beard to go to the cinema is true – but if things go wrong they become the lowest of the low. Having Greg Chappell there will help, because he is great to talk to re cricket.

With the Indian team you have a pretty good idea of who and what you will be facing. In Pakistan it can be guesswork, varying from one week to the next depending on the direction of the wind. Captains and coaches seem to come through revolving doors. They have had some outstanding players in my time but also suffered some terrible defeats. In Sharjah in 2002 we bowled them out for 59 and 53 and, while we bowled pretty well, a side as good as Pakistan should not be collapsing like that twice in the same Test. This after their coach Richard Pybus had said that Australia were coming to the end of an era. It must be stated though we batted first, they were in the field for a day in 55°C heat. Matty Hayden made a brilliant hundred.

I have never understood why Pakistan have been unable to play spin as well as their neighbours. The Indians are the best in the world and with plenty of slow bowlers in Pakistan as well there is no reason why their batsmen should be inferior. Mushtaq Ahmed and Saqlain Mushtaq were an effective pair and the inspirational Abdul Qadir is still around to coach the kids. And they now have a very useful and aggressive leggie in Danish Kaneria. Generally, though, the Pakistanis are slower and less decisive at the crease. They have never struck me as confident and when they want to be aggressive it seems to be pre-meditated – they run down the pitch whether the ball is there to be hit or not. Because they have so much natural ability, perhaps they don't spend enough time thinking about a plan. Over the years I have got to know the way they play, but even some of their most experienced batsmen don't seem a great deal wiser against leg-spin than when I bowled to them for the first time. Of all the countries, my record is worst against India and best against Pakistan – 90 wickets in 15 Tests at an average of around 20.

> With the Indian team you have a pretty good idea of who and what you will be facing. In Pakistan it can be guesswork.

> The Indians are the best in the world and with plenty of slow bowlers in Pakistan as well, there is no reason why their batsmen should be inferior.

Looking back, they may have slightly under-achieved over the past 15 years. Wasim Akram and Waqar Younis formed one of the all-time great attacks. They were both quick and Wasim being left-arm and whippy gave them something unique in the game. There should not have been anything to stop a side with two bowlers of that quality, but apart from 1994-95 – the series when Salim Malik was investigated – it did not happen for them against us. There were always reports of squabbles in the dressing room. I assumed they just thrived on that chaos.

Sri Lanka, on the other hand, have preferred to squabble with everybody else. Perhaps that statement is a little unfair these days but it is certainly a fair reflection on Arjuna Ranatunga's time as captain. And he still likes to have his say now in team stuff, as most ex-players do to be honest; but he really needs to let it go. In my playing career, he was arguably the one player in world cricket that could raise the hackles. Everyone can accept batsmen scoring runs and always try to applaud a hundred. If a guy has some luck along the way, then that is part of the game. But I didn't accept Ranatunga stretching the rules, without breaking them, to suit a game plan.

> Of all the countries, my record is worst against India and best against Pakistan – 90 wickets in 15 Tests at an average of around 20.

There was one occasion where he refused to shake hands with us after a one-day game. He should have shown more respect to players and opponents, but that is the way it can sometimes be in high pressure games.

Whenever he wasn't around, and since his retirement, games against Sri Lanka have been played in a much better atmosphere, even though they are still a bit too quick to complain on occasions. Just because I have a low opinion of Ranatunga doesn't mean I have a problem with Sri Lanka. It is one of my favourite countries and the people some of the most charming. My first Australia tour was there in 1992 and it was unfortunate that security issues meant we could not play in Colombo during the 1996 World Cup. In my case, a death-threat warning me not to go was delivered by hand to my parents' home. The Test match at SSC in 1992 is still my favourite even after 140-odd games.

We have toured twice since and the 2004 series was special as it marked the end of my enforced lay-off. During the year away all sorts of thoughts had crossed my mind but I was determined to go on playing and try to make up the lost time. I worked hard on my fitness and my bowling in the two months before the trip, but I couldn't have dreamt how well

Cricket can seem pretty insignificant in the grand scheme of life but I am very fortunate because I can use my profile to draw attention to more important causes.

I would go with ten wickets in each of the first two Tests at Galle and Kandy, and 26 in the series overall. We finished at the Sinhalese ground in Colombo where I made my first serious contribution for Australia 12 years earlier. Both were tight finishes.

In 2005 I went over for a few days to help raise funds for the Tsunami Appeal. I had asked Muttiah Muralitharan whether I could do anything to help. He said that just meeting people and generating publicity would be greatly appreciated. Galle held very special memories for me: it was my first game back after my suspension and I also took my 500th wicket there. The ground had been badly hit by the tsunami. We visited one village nearby that was run by a man called Kashil who was also Murali's manager. He ran a wonderful little place that educated children and it was very badly destroyed. The kids had lost their family, possessions, everything except hope that better times lay ahead. It was unbelievable to see with your own eyes.

One of the proudest achievements in my life has been to set up the Shane Warne Foundation, a charity aimed at helping seriously ill and under-privileged children. We are really only in Australia at present but want to take it to the world. Cricket can seem pretty insignificant in the grand scheme of life but I am very fortunate because I can use my profile to draw attention to more important causes. If we organise a dinner with some good speakers, give people a fun night out and raise some money, then we are all doing our bit to help.

I have got to know Murali better since the tsunami. In my time I don't think one player has been as important to his team as he is to Sri Lanka.

I have got to know Murali better since the tsunami. In my time I don't think one player has been as important to his team as he is to Sri Lanka. There will be a big gap in the side when he retires. It is understandable that people will compare us because we are both spinners and we are the leading wicket-takers in Test cricket. I have been lucky to play in a side with excellent pace bowlers so I do not have to carry the attack in the same way as

Murali. True, Chaminda Vaas can be dangerous, but he is not in the same league as Glenn McGrath. For as long as he plays I can see Murali continuing to bowl nearly half of Sri Lanka's overs and therefore take half of their wickets. My guess is that he will finish with about 1,000 Test wickets, for what that is worth.

Test Cricket is strong at the moment and that's why I believe that Bangladesh should not be playing Test cricket in any case, and the same goes for Zimbabwe. I strongly believe that Test cricket should be of a certain standard, and that anything less just weakens the brand. Any country can play badly in the odd game or even slip below their normal standard during a series because of injuries and the like. But the fact is that Bangladesh are being beaten heavily time after time, and the same goes for Zimbabwe: if they play one-day cricket, hopefully they will improve enough eventually to reach Test standard.

Most of the time averages never tell the full story, but in some cases they are starting to flatter certain players.

It cannot be right that statistics from Kerry Packer's great World Series Cricket matches, which featured the best players in the world, go unrecognised while those involving Bangladesh carry Test status. Records are being discredited as bowlers take cheap wickets and batsmen score easy runs. Most of the time averages never tell the full story but in some cases they are starting to flatter certain players. But you can work stats to back whatever argument you want, and paint any picture that you want.

I am trying to be kind to Bangladesh here and suggest the best way to become a decent Test side, because that is what all of us want. I just don't think the way ahead is to keep placing their young players in situations where they are out of their depth. That way they will learn how to lose and not a lot else. It must be better from them to face A teams, or state and county opponents when they go away on tour. They need to take that step backwards to be able to re-enter Test cricket more confidently in the future – my opinion only. I'm all for spreading the word but not to the detriment of Test cricket and the brand.

This is when cricket started to become serious – my Test debut for Australia against India at Sydney in 1992, and still the proudest moment of my career. Not that it was a fairy-tale introduction. I dropped Ravi Shastri on 66 and he went on to score a double-hundred. At least I got him out in the end. This was the third match of the series and I'd been at the second as a spectator enjoying a few beers with some mates in the pavilion. Times were about to change.

The anguished look only begins to tell this story as a ball to Inzamam-ul-Haq beats Ian Healy to give Pakistan the four byes they needed to beat us by one wicket in Karachi in 1994. The night before, included Malik talking to Tim May and I in the conversation which later blew up into the globally publicised allegation of a bribery offer to us. It's history now that we lost the game anyway without needing any external inducement, and we left that match without any affection for that player.

I didn't need much motivation when Salim Malik and Pakistan came to Australia in 1995. Whatever I'm saying here to the bloke it probably wasn't "good luck mate." The investigation into bribery allegations in 1994 has been discussed at length, so I won't bore you with the details. Needless to say though, we won the series 2-1 – I think the result was justice of a sort.

Games between Australia and Sri Lanka were already becoming eventful before Darrell Hair no-balled Muttiah Muralitharan for throwing at the Boxing Day Test in 1995. I was in the pavilion at the time and it took me a while to realise what was happening. Murali's action looks unusual but the ICC say he is okay, so we all know where we stand. My concern is that young kids – without the same deformity Murali has in his elbow – may try to copy their hero and find that their arm does straighten illegally.

next pages
Murali has become a good friend down the years – there is something of a union among spin bowlers. As usual, he's smiling in this picture. I have never thought of us in a race to finish our careers with more Test wickets, but if other people want to bill it like that then I guess it generates interest in the game. I actually think Murali could end with close to 1,000 simply because he bowls so many overs.

I'm at first slip here as Adam Gilchrist catches Ijaz Ahmed off Glenn McGrath at Brisbane in 1999. The game is remembered as Gilchrist's debut and there was some controversy because Ian Healy wanted to play at his home ground. Gilchrist had become a fixture as an opener in the one-day side and the way he batted helped us to take the game to another level. Quite simply one great player replaced another – the handshake here almost marks the transition – and we won this series against Pakistan comfortably.

We went into the Calcutta Test in 2001
on the back of a record 16 successive
wins and it took an amazing innings
by VVS Laxman to bring that run to
an end. At the time, his 281 was the
highest Test score for India. We had
made them follow on but my abiding
memory is of Laxman just whipping
ball after ball through midwicket
against the spin. It must have been
great to watch and it was certainly
the innings of his life. India became
the last frontier for us and we lost the
series 2-1. It was another three years
before we reversed that scoreline.

This is one of those captions that
probably ought to read, "Shane Warne
feels the heat". Even with ice-cold
water, a cooling crystal neck scarf
and a thick wristband you can see the
sweat on my forehead. This was
Sharjah in 2002 when our series
against Pakistan was switched because
of security issues. Temperatures
reached 50°C in the middle – you can
go off for rain but that kind of heat is
more dangerous. Given the conditions,
I was delighted to take 27 wickets in
our 3-0 win.

What a difference a year makes. In March 2004 Hashan Tillekeratne became my 500th Test wicket at the beautiful ground in Galle, famous for the old fort in the background. When I visited 11 months later the stadium had been devastated in the Boxing Day tsunami and those happy memories seemed a world away. Muttiah Muralitharan and other players helped with the relief effort and I was keen to go over there to see if I could do my bit. Putting smiles on the faces of kids who had lost everything in the disaster was a humbling experience.

Rain in Chennai prevented a good finish to the second Test of our 2004 series against India but not before I overtook Muttiah Muralitharan as the leading wicket-taker of all time – Irfan Pathan becoming victim number 533 thanks to a typically sharp slip catch by Matty Hayden. The cheering seemed to go on forever in the stands. They were such a sporting crowd. One statistician worked out it had taken 31,887 balls to get to the record; no wonder my body is falling apart.

For his range of shots and consistency despite pressure in India that you can hardly begin to imagine, I would rate Sachin Tendulkar as the best batsmen I've faced. He gets in to position so quickly – to cut, for example, as he is doing here in Chennai. What people maybe don't appreciate is the hours of effort he puts in. We were both fortunate to be invited to Sir Donald Bradman's 90th birthday and it was fascinating to hear Sachin talk to the great man about technique. In 2005 we were again on opposite sides in a fund-raising match for the Tsunami Appeal.

The 1980s would have gone down as
a dark age for leg-spin had it not been
for Abdul Qadir. He was one of the
players I used to imitate as a kid in
my back garden, though in real games
my own short approach was very
different to his bouncing run-up.
I remember spending an evening at
his house in Lahore during our 1994
tour, just talking about spin and
flipping different balls to each other
across the floor of his living room.

I like to think I've made a lot of friends
in cricket but sadly, Arjuna Ranatunga
and I have not exactly seen eye to eye.
As captain of Sri Lanka I felt he took
liberties with the spirit of the game. He
pushed the rules as hard as he could
sometimes, which some would argue
was unacceptable. Some people
thought he was good for Sri Lanka. Yes,
they achieved success under him, but
there were also times when he held
their progression back.

CHAPTER FIVE

SOUTH AFRICA

Of all the international sides, South Africa are very hard to beat but at the same time I never feel worried about them taking us apart. I think it comes down to personality. In general they are very regimented and disciplined people, with discipline being their strength. They are polite, respectful and tough. What they lack is that bit of flair and imagination that leaves you as an opponent scratching your head and struggling to think of a Plan B, and against the best players you need Plan A all the way to Z, and sometimes that's not enough.

Games against South Africa can be attritional affairs. You must wear them down gradually, especially when they are at home. They might not score at a quick rate by modern standards but they do not lie down and give you wickets when they fall behind either. Nor do their bowlers have those mad half-hours when they lose all control of line and length.

Hansie Cronje was probably their most imaginative captain and he got the best out of his players. Kepler Wessels set the standard for the players and Graeme Smith is learning the hard way. I feel there is something lacking under Smith at the moment. They do not seem to play as one unit. When he brought his side to Australia in 2005-06 I think he decided that his best chance of success was to be confrontational. This, to me, does not suit their style of play. As results continued to go our way I think he made himself look a little silly. I wonder if some of his colleagues were a bit embarrassed by that approach. We won the series 2-0 and it would have been 3-0 but for a determined hundred by Jacques Rudolph on the final day at Perth.

My first visit in 1993-94 was a real eye-opener. Australia had not toured for nearly 25 years and from the moment we landed there was so much hype about the series. Thousands of people seemed to want an autograph or a photo of the players. The profile can be nice, but

I have no hesitation in saying that South Africa is a great place to tour. I understand that crowds are going to be hostile and aggressive.

some of the people were quite rude and it became obtrusive on occasions. I was still young and wasn't sure how to deal with it all. I was lucky to have guys like Merv, AB and the rest of the senior players to look after me and the other young players.

I have no hesitation – none – in saying that South Africa is a great place to tour. I understand that crowds are going to be hostile and aggressive. There is nothing wrong with wanting your own side to win. It is up to senior players such as myself to let the first-time tourists know what they will be up against. Of all the places we go, South Africa is closest to the Australian climate. The beaches are wonderful and the game parks an incredible experience. As for the vineyards, I always think of Merv Hughes who christened Stellenbosch, "Still on the Booze".

In the early days their side was a mix of players who must have wondered whether they would ever get a chance to play international cricket because of apartheid and youngsters such as Allan Donald and Jonty Rhodes. Back then and since, they have not had a spinner I would describe as world class. Paul Adams presented a challenge for a while because his style was unorthodox, but once batsmen grew used to his action and the way his stock ball turned, he lost his early potency and returned to domestic cricket.

Big Pat Symcox was more defensive, and when they have picked a spinner recently it has tended to be Nicky Boje. He is a handy all-round player with a couple of one-day hundreds who often goes in as low as number nine in Tests. When he started, he was a quite aggressive spin bowler. Perhaps spin, with its mystery, just doesn't suit their character. Mind you, captains need to understand their spinners to get the best out of them. The attack tends to be a combination of tall, right-arm medium-fast bowlers who put it on a length. As a unit there is not a lot of subtlety or variation.

I don't want to sound like I am dissing South Africa because they have produced some excellent players.

Australia had not toured for nearly 25 years and from the moment we landed there was so much hype about the series.

> **Brian McMillan was the best all-rounder in the world for a couple of years and Kallis reached the same heights until his knees hindered his bowling.**

There are not many harder batsmen to dismiss than Jacque Kallis. Gary Kirsten was another I admired. He was a brave opener and a dream for his own bowlers. They could toil all day knowing Kirsten would not undo their hard work with a rash shot.

Brian McMillan was the best all-rounder in the world for a couple of years and Kallis reached the same heights until his knees hindered his bowling. I tend to think of Shaun Pollock slightly differently, as a very good seam and swing bowler who can also bat. For the past ten years he has been their equivalent of our Glenn McGrath, a bloke who has the discipline to create pressure by putting the ball on the spot. It is strange that Australia have rarely used a traditional all-rounder in my time. I think the thing with all-rounders is that their batting average must be higher than their bowling. And everyone tries to compare all-rounders.

Since the last Ashes series our selectors seem to have adopted a change in strategy and consciously picked an all-rounder. Shane Watson came into the side straight away but lost his place because of injury. Then, rather than go back to a sixth specialist batsman, like Michael Clarke who is good for a few overs here and there, anyway, they chose Andrew Symonds. You couldn't find a more versatile cricketer. Symonds can bat, field and bowl seam or off-spin depending on the conditions. I think to succeed in the long term he will need to show he is very good in one area, but he has the talent to be a match-winning batsman, and his bowling as the 4th seamer can be very handy.

> **Hansie was much-admired in the dressing room, and his sad passing hit them really hard.**

If he goes on to play a few years of Test cricket he may look back on the Melbourne Test against South Africa as a turning point. We needed some quick runs in the second innings and although that would seem to be a tailor-made situation for Symonds, he was under pressure of knowing he had to perform. He hit six sixes and scored 72 from 54 balls in all – just what was wanted. His innings knocked the South Africans back and we bowled them out quite easily in the fourth innings. His batting flowed into his bowling, and he took some valuable wickets too.

By the start of 2006 and up to the tour of Bangladesh, we had won ten out of eleven Test matches. The selectors made a few changes after we lost to England, but I think it is clear we are moving in the right direction. The biggest plus was the introduction of Mike Hussey at number five. He is one of those guys who just loves batting, and has performed unbelievably well.

In England a few people have suggested we are in denial about the Ashes, and building ourselves up again as though the series did not happen. That is just nonsense. We had a period where we thought about what had happened, looked at our own games and tried to improve. I think England are going to have to be at their best again to beat us. Cricket Australia also took a few things on board to see if our preparations could be more effective. One result was that we managed to bring Troy Cooley back home as bowling coach. But there comes a point where you have to move on. Bruce Reid is another coach who I'm sure was in the running. And I think our response in the 2005-06 season showed that we've done just that. Believe me, I haven't forgotten the disappointment at losing the Ashes just because I don't keep talking about it. I've said "Congratulations" thousands of times.

As for South Africa, they pushed us particularly close around the turn of the decade, especially in the one-day game. Hansie was much-admired in the dressing room, and his sad passing hit them really hard, which is understandable as he was a big influence on them. I'm sure this group of South Africans will not like being rated as the sixth-best team in Tests. Whether the quota system has had a harmful effect, I am not qualified to say. But I do believe in picking your best team at all times. Having seen some of the work in the townships I am sure kids from under-privileged backgrounds will break through, as long as investment continues and the coaching is right. The 2005-06 touring team were not as good as some of their predecessors but I am sure the talent and enthusiasm is still there in the country.

> Having seen some of the work in the townships, I am sure kids from under-privileged backgrounds will break through, as long as investment continues and the coaching is right.

I'm in among that lot somewhere, celebrating after Neil McKenzie became my 100th South African Test wicket at Durban in 2002. This was the third and final match of the series. We were already 2-0 up and the fact that South Africa scored 340 to win, on a flat pitch, tells me they are at their best when the pressure is off. They had nothing to lose. In a tight situation I would always back Australia to beat them.

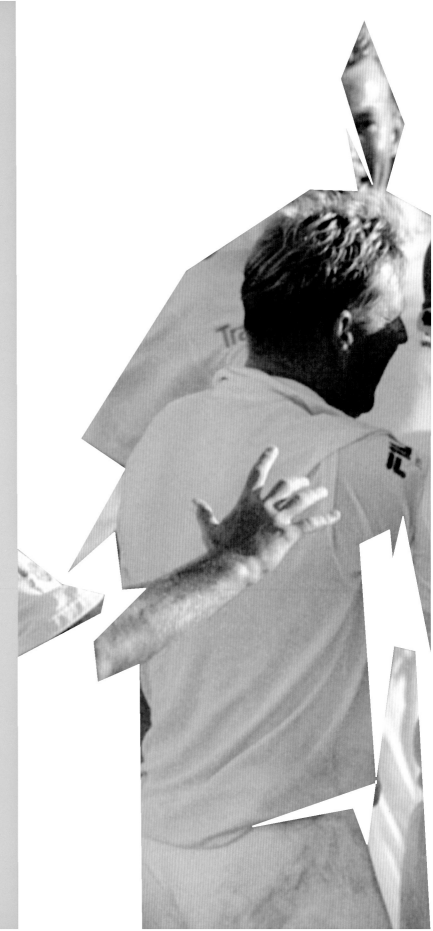

Jonty Rhodes became one of my best mates in the South Africa team. He was such an enthusiastic player that his influence on the side went beyond statistics – especially in the one-day game. Jonty would always be the one lifting them in the field when the chips were down and he could inspire his bowlers with a brilliant stop. I am not sure that personality has been replaced. South Africa were lucky to have such a good role model for kids when they came back into the international game.

Despite all the wear and tear on my
shoulders and fingers I managed to get
through to 100 Tests and the occasion
at Cape Town in 2002 was particularly
special because Brooke and Jackson
were there with me. They certainly saw
plenty of their daddy in action –
I bowled 70 overs in the second innings
and 98 in the match. This was one of
our best wins in my time as an
Australia player because we chased
334 to win on the last day.

Sometimes you can bowl a spell where the force is really with you. Here is a case in point, Sydney 1994. The pitch is always great for spinners and this time it started to turn on the very first afternoon. At one point I had figures of 7 for 28 from 15 overs including this caught and bowled to get rid of Kepler Wessels. Overall I finished with 12 for 128 – still my best match return 12 years on. But the story had an unhappy ending as we were bowled out for 111 to lose by five runs. Damien Martyn copped most of the flak and it took him a long time to get back into the side.

This was my 100th Test wicket – Brian McMillan done by a flipper. By this point I felt I had started to master that particular ball. During the first part of my career McMillan was probably the best all-rounder in the world. He could be an intimidating figure, but you could also get under his skin. We christened him 'Depardieu' after the French actor with the big nose. He didn't like that. After our narrow defeat at Sydney we were pumped to win here in Adelaide to take the series.

Whoever described the Wanderers ground in Johannesburg as the Bull Ring deserves a prize because I can't think of a more appropriate nickname. In 1994 I got into a lot of trouble for giving Andrew Hudson a pretty unpleasant send-off after bowling him round his legs. I was like a kettle waiting to boil over, having been on the wrong end of abuse from the crowd. When we returned three years later I spoke at the team meeting about the blood-thirsty atmosphere we could expect. We won by an innings and the crowd were a bit quieter. Here, Hudson struggles to make his ground.

Daryll Cullinan bowled for a duck at Melbourne in 1997. I gave him a terrible time down the years. He set himself up for a fall with his sledging from slip but when he batted himself things got worse and worse. At one point he went to a psychiatrist to help deal with leg-spin. I hope for his sake he played it better from the couch. His record against everybody else was fine, but he never got over his phobia against Australia.

A memorable wicket in a memorable game for me – Jacques Kallis, my 11th wicket of the Sydney Test in 1998 and the 300th of my career. It was about this time that Ian Healy compared the South African batsmen to rabbits trapped in headlights. As wicketkeeper he had the best view of all, so I wasn't in a position to disagree. Kallis was still relatively inexperienced at this stage of his career. I set him up with a series of leg-breaks from around the wicket before bowling him with a top-spinner as he padded up.

Perth has not been an especially happy ground for me personally but there was something to remember in 2005. This wicket – Ashwell Prince leg-before to a big leg-break with Brad Hodge and Adam Gilchrist joining in the appeal – took me past Dennis Lillee's record of 85 for a calendar year. At moments like that you have to pinch yourself because Lillee is one of the all-time greats. I loved his image – the long, black hair and dark eyes boring through a batsman.

The match-fixing issue has been the biggest controversy to hit cricket in my time. We played in South Africa in 2000 only a few days after Hansie Cronje – here giving evidence to the King Commission – confessed to dealing with bookmakers. I was as surprised as anybody. Cronje was a very tough competitor. He always appeared to give 100 percent and hated losing. His early death ended a very, very sad story.

next pages
When South Africa came over in 2005-06 I'm sure Graeme Smith made a conscious decision to try to scare us with big statements. He wanted to portray himself as a strong, aggressive captain. I don't have a problem with that, but you have to back it up with action and the plain fact is that Smith fell short. We were certainly not going to back down and a few words were exchanged over the matches, not least here at Melbourne.

CHAPTER SIX

WEST INDIES

When I grew up playing cricket there was no doubt about the best side in the world. West Indies, with their super-charged battery of fast bowlers and dashing batsmen, had led the way for more than a decade and were showing little sign of giving way. The tables have been well and truly turned since then and those great days seem a lifetime away.

Although we beat them 3-0 at the end of 2005 they showed signs of being over the worst. They fought hard and showed a lot of spirit and have a few talented young players. As long as younger players like Dwayne Bravo get the guidance they need, I don't see why the new generation cannot start to challenge properly. It is a big ask for them to regain their former glory, and they can do without the pressure of trying to match the great players of the past.

But the fact is that cricket needs a strong West Indies with their flair and spark – the one thing they do is entertain.

> I have always enjoyed bowling to their batsmen. Most of them fit in to one of two categories: they are either blockers or smashers.

It is hard to know where they went wrong. I think you have to look at the opposition as well and give Australia, for one, some credit. The rest of the world eventually caught up. Having been top of the pile for so long it must have been easy to think the conveyor belt of talent would keep rolling along without having to look for new parts. But when we finally beat them in 1995 their aura of invincibility slipped. It was bound to happen at some stage and by standing up to them through four amazing Test matches Australia showed what could be done.

The fact is that cricket needs a strong West Indies with their flair and spark – the one thing they do is entertain.

That was possibly one of the best series I was involved in until last year's Ashes. Before the start we made a conscious decision not to be intimidated by their fast bowlers. We knew they would pepper our batsmen, including the lower order, so we decided to fight fire with fire. In the past, sides had gone easy on their tail-enders hoping they would cut out their own short stuff in return. Fat chance! Our build-up was centred around the short ball – how to bowl it effectively on the one hand and how to sway out of the way on the other. Even our net sessions, with short ball after short ball, people were getting hit. Mark Waugh and Ricky Ponting are two of the best bumper bowlers in the nets.

It took a lot of courage on our part to come through, not least when Steve Waugh went face-to-face with Ambrose in Trinidad on one of the worst pitches I've ever seen for a Test match. I realised Ambrose meant business when he produced a ball that chipped my right thumb not long afterwards, but we all gritted out those few weeks and won the final decisive Test in Jamaica by an innings. I think Richie Richardson, their captain, made a bit of a fool of himself when he described us as the worst Australian team he had faced. That was not saying much about his team.That was out of character because he is a good guy. His words betrayed the pressure he was under at the time.

It is important for a bowler to know his role and fit in with the overall plan. We bowl in pairs just as batsmen operate in partnerships. This time my task was to offer variety and try to keep things tight while

We knew they would pepper our batsmen, including the lower order, so we decided to fight fire with fire.

the ball was darting around at the other end. West Indies have lacked the same balance in their attack. With four quick bowlers they probably never thought they were missing anything. In the past few years, though, they could have used somebody to offer control.

I have always enjoyed bowling to their batsmen. Most of them fit in to one of two categories: they are either blockers or smashers. As a bowler you can either build up pressure with dot balls or spin up and try to force a mistake from somebody looking to attack. A guy like Chris

This time my task was to offer variety and try to keep things tight while the ball was darting around at the other end.

Gayle can be a dream to watch. There are also times when he will cause his team-mates and the public to tear their hair out. I am all for batsmen playing their natural game but there does have to be half a nod towards the state of the game.

Brian Lara has been an exception. He is the best left-hander I have bowled to by quite a way. Like all great batsmen he gets into position that split-second earlier than the rest to give himself more scoring options. Even with some big fourth-innings totals to defend I've never thought a game is won with Lara at the crease. Captains talk about the 'Lara factor' when they set a declaration. He became the leading Test run-scorer of all time despite a tonne-weight of expectation on his shoulders. At times he has practically carried the side and his batting against us in the 1998-99 series was just phenomenal. He has an unbelievable eye and his placement sets him apart from the rest.

I dread to think what might have happened to the West Indies without Lara. There were even reports of basketball and soccer taking over in popularity as the defeats mounted. Having been there a few times and seen the passion for cricket I'm not so sure, but you cannot be complacent in an age when there are so many more opportunities for kids. People there are very proud and Lara gave them something to be proud about when the rest of their side was falling apart. When they start moving up the Test rankings they will thank Lara for keeping the torch alight during some difficult years. Their young players are hopefully picking his brains.

There were times when I found it hard to think of Curtly Ambrose and Courtney Walsh doing me a favour.

With more and more computer technology and too many coaching programmes around, people have to keep using their brains, not rely on that rubbish. That will always be a start, of course. I remember once asking Jimmy Adams, a West Indian captain and a gentleman of the game, why some of their players were reluctant to dive to save runs in the outfield. He explained that they were not accustomed to doing that at home where the grounds were rough and would tear open their arms. It is hard to learn without good pitches and facilities.

West Indies played a major part in my development. Odd though it sounds, my swift promotion from state cricket in the late 80s and early 90s owed something to their great pace bowlers. There were times when I found it hard to think of Curtly Ambrose and Courtney Walsh doing me a favour. But the Australia selectors worked out that to topple the champions required something different. There were not many leggies around in those days, especially with Abdul Qadir moving towards the end of his career, and despite being raw I could spin the ball a long way. They thought I might be able to pose a new threat.

The Caribbean is a fantastic place to tour. I toured there in 1990 for the first time. They are passionate about their cricket and have a good knowledge of the game. They like to be entertained and soon let a batsman know if he is going too slowly. In other circumstances I can imagine being among them in my shorts and sandals, dizzy with a large rum and coke and shouting at the players to get a move on. With grounds being re-developed for the 2007 World Cup, I hope their distinctive characters remain. It promises to be the mother of all parties. I hope I'm there ... not playing.

> The Caribbean is a fantastic place to tour. I toured there in 1990 for the first time. They are passionate about their cricket and have a good knowledge of the game.

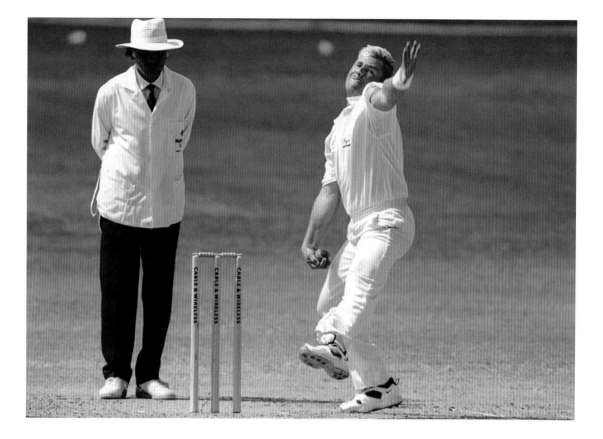

The Melbourne Test of 1992 was one of
the most important of my career –
maybe the most important of all. Going
in to the final day some of the papers
were speculating this might be my last
chance. Everything was in my favour –
home ground, a worn pitch and
batsmen on the chase. Fortunately
I came up trumps. Richie Richardson is
in full flow here but when I deceived
him with a flipper the game began to
turn. I finished with 7 for 52 and felt I'd
answered a few questions.

above
To beat West Indies in Barbados in 1995
ranks as a great performance, not just
because of the quality of the opposition
but because of injuries in our own
camp. Our coach Bobby Simpson was
admitted to hospital with thrombosis
during the game. It was clear that the
likes of Carl Hooper wanted to get after
me and my ears are probably still
ringing with the sound of horns and
cow bells from the stands as the runs
flowed. I came back, took five wickets
in the match and between us we laid
a marker for a titanic series.

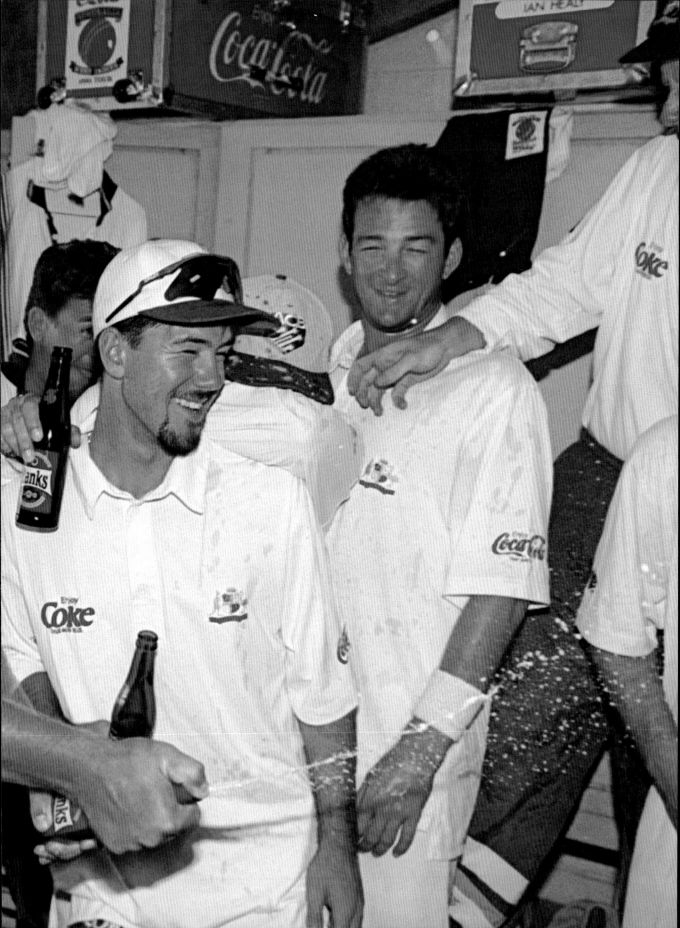

The third Test in Trinidad was the scariest of my life. The pitch was green and damp and something had clearly annoyed Curtly Ambrose. He was an angry man from first to last. At one point Richie Richardson had to drag him away when he squared up to Steve Waugh. I was left with a hand the size of a boxing glove after being struck. At the other end I nicked one from Courtney Walsh only for the umpire to call a no ball. According to Paul Reiffel at the non-striker's end I actually cried: "Oh, no!"

At last! This was the huddle after I took the last wicket of the fourth Test in Jamaica to win the 1995 series 2-1. We beat them by an innings here and Steve Waugh added to his reputation with a double-hundred. The Tests had been hyped as a battle between myself and Brian Lara, but the situation meant that everybody played a part. The scale of the task helped us to gel and when things got nasty the squad just grew closer.

By the mid-point of the 1995 Test series we were ready for a break. We had a practice game in St Kitts and while we were on the island we decided to dress up in our whites and head off to the top of a cliff for a team picture with a difference. When you look at the scenery behind us you appreciate why the West Indies is such a wonderful place to tour.

After the series the wives and girlfriends flew out to join us for a few days in Bermuda. I think there may have been some low-key cricket as well but I must confess I don't remember much of it. The word on all our lips was 'party' and there isn't a better place than the Caribbean if that's what you want. Our Board said they would pay for a night out on the back of our triumph. We ate caviar, drank champagne and the bill came to $13,000.

Just as Muttiah Muralitharan and myself are stretching the record for most Test wickets, I can see a battle between Brian Lara and Sachin Tendulkar to finish as leading run scorer. This is Brian at Adelaide in 2005 when he passed Allan Border's total of 11,174. He might have made his highest scores against England but his best performances have been against us. I remember an innings of 277 at Sydney in 1993 in particular. In the end it took a run out to remove him.

Everybody in the Caribbean wants West Indies to return to former glories and that puts a lot of pressure on young players coming through. They need time and a run in the side to find their way and can't be expected to become match-winners overnight. But during the 2005 series I could see the shoots of a recovery. Dwayne Bravo looked especially promising – not least when I drove back this ball at Adelaide and saw him hold an instinctive, athletic catch. Definitely one to watch.

next pages
Although first slip has become my position when the pace bowlers are operating, I'm not so used to fielding there against the spinners. It tends to be me bowling at the other end, with Matty Hayden at slip. The ball can come at all heights and angles in a split-second and for a big bloke Matty takes some very athletic catches. I was pleased with this one myself – Denesh Ramdin taken low down off Stuart MacGill at Hobart in 2005.

CHAPTER SEVEN

NEW ZEALAND

I have always had a lot of time for New Zealand and have enjoyed playing them. Considering their relatively small pool of players they have produced some wonderful players and they often reserve their best for Australia. I think they see us as their biggest rivals, whereas our leading series is always the Ashes. But that is no slight against the Black Caps. With a good captain, thorough planning and that willingness to have a go all the way down the order, they have earned absolute respect.

Stephen Fleming has shown that you can lead by example without making a song and dance on the pitch or big statements off it. He has an easy-going temperament but he wants to win as badly as the next man. Being so popular helps to bring out the best in his team, and I was surprised that Graeme Smith was chosen above him to captain the ICC World XI in the Super Series in 2005. They are both tall and left-handed, but there I would suggest the similarities end. The first person picked should be the captain, then work your way down.

Their problem has always been to find 11 players to contribute consistently. For a start, they have struggled to find a long-term opening partnership. On the bowling side, Shane Bond has had a lot of bad luck with injury when he should have been leading the attack. Chris Cairns was another struck by injuries too often. As for the spin department, Dan Vettori has had to bowl a lot of overs and I know from experience how that takes its toll.

New Zealand have also been good at thinking outside the box.

As a one-day unit they can be a match for any side. Perhaps the fact that they do not have big reserves means that players have to come through as multi-skilled. Guys like Chris Harris, Jacob Oram and Scott Styris have been ideal for the shorter game because they can score quick runs and bowl a good allocation. That doesn't mean they're not effective at Test cricket – they have been. New Zealand have also been good at thinking outside the box. In the mid-90s they had a group of slow-medium bowlers who would have a lot of discipline and bowl line and length over after over, and were effective in their own way. Then there was the brave decision to open the bowling with Dipak Patel's off-spin during the 1992 World Cup.

> As a one-day unit they can be a match for any side. Perhaps the fact that they do not have big reserves means that players have to come through as multi-skilled.

When they came close to giving us a scare and probably should have won towards the end of 2001 it was through good planning and some very brave cricket. Stephen Fleming has to take credit here – he got in our faces, and played excellent aggressive cricket. Under his captaincy New Zealand have played fantastic and exciting cricket.

We seem to meet more than ever before these days. I am all for doing what I can for the region as a whole and we are natural allies. New Zealand is a fantastic place to tour, as long as you remember to pack a scarf and a warm jumper. It does not present us with an immediate culture shock. The scenery is beautiful and even in the cities there is no great rush about life. My only concern is that the frequency of games may leave spectators in both countries wanting less. I would also say that New Zealand have to make sure that their pitches are good enough to allow a proper balance between bat and ball. The surface we used for a Tsunami Appeal game at Hamilton in 2005 was terrible and some of the others have not been a lot better.

> New Zealand is a fantastic place to tour, as long as you remember to pack a scarf and a warm jumper.

For all that, I have enjoyed bowling against them. The first series against them in 1993 was especially important for me because it was scheduled immediately before the Ashes tour. Until then I'd enjoyed some good moments but had not really performed consistently throughout a series. This time I made a big effort to improve my fitness – I even cut out pizza for a while. The three Tests taught me that hard work does bring reward and meant that I could go to England with confidence.

By the time we next met I had established a good partnership with Tim May. The combination of a leggie or left-arm spinner with an off-break bowler can be very effective because the stock balls turn in opposite directions. However, the pair of us had other things on our minds when New Zealand came over in 1997-98. More and more money was coming into the game and, as players, we felt we were not getting our fair share. The disagreement resulted in a serious problem with the Board. I was secretary of the Cricketers' Association while Tim was one of our main negotiators. Fortunately we did not have to carry out our threat to strike, but it was a pretty unpleasant time.

> We seem to meet more than ever before these days. I am all for doing what I can for the region as a whole and we are natural allies.

The home series against New Zealand in 1993 was our first since arriving back in England with the Ashes retained. There were receptions in Sydney and Melbourne and I'd even been invited onto the field before the AFL Grand Final. With all of this new attention I wanted to keep the momentum going so it was nice to take wickets in the second Test here at Hobart. The first game had not gone so well but the selectors then recalled Tim May – my favourite spin partner down the years.

This is a wicket I'll always remember – Paul Wiseman out sweeping in Auckland in 2000. It took me past Dennis Lillee's record of 355 wickets for an Australian bowler and the great man was one of the first to send a note saying, "Well done". It's funny looking at the picture to see how far I ran down the pitch in excitement before Adam Gilchrist took the catch. The record had been at the back of my mind and I wasn't bowling too well. In fact it seemed I would have to wait for the next Test to get to 356. Wiseman was the last wicket of the game, and I could clink the champagne glasses afterwards with my brother and my dad after all.

An image I like to see – driving the ball back past Dan Vettori. I've nothing at all against Vettori as a bloke. He just happens to have dismissed me more times in Test cricket than any other bowler. Spinners tend to do well because I like to try to hit them out of the ground! Dan is an old-fashioned spinner who relies on degrees of spin and flight rather than the mystery of a 'doosra', which is very hard to bowl without straightening the arm. He has been a great servant for New Zealand either as a stock or strike bowler – and sometimes both at once.

I've been out to Vettori on nine
occasions and none as annoying as this
– caught on 99 attempting to hit over
midwicket at Perth in 2001. I played over
the moment time and time again that
night. Why couldn't I be Steve Waugh
for once in my life, take the safe option
and push it somewhere for a single?
Mark Richardson gives me a pat on the
back in this picture; he was the bloke
who took the catch. You soon pick
yourself up, and I'm determined to get
that Test hundred one day.

Chris Martin is leg-before at Brisbane
in 2004, sealing an innings victory.
The Gabba is not generally reckoned to
be a great ground for spinners, but it is
one of my favourite in Australia. I took
eight wickets in this match and I've
generally been successful there down
the years. It is a good ground to judge
a player because you always get an
even contest. I remember this particular
game not just because of New
Zealand's second innings collapse but
a brilliant hundred by Michael Clarke.

This is my 1,000th first-class wicket, taken in Christchurch in 2005. It wasn't simply the landmark that made it more than usually satisfying. Hamish Marshall had scored 146 in the first innings, so he'd enjoyed a good look at my bowling. Despite that I still managed to bowl him through his legs later in the game when he decided not to offer a shot to a big leg-spinner. Players are given bats for a reason so I never have any sympathy when they use their pads instead.

Stephen Fleming – here in action against India – is the best opposition captain I've come across as well as being an elegant and probably under-rated batsman. There was a lot of expectation when he took on the job at a young age but he made sure he went about the task his own way. New Zealand teams have generally been a lot happier with him in charge. He always presents a good face in public where he talks honestly but without criticising his team.

Chris Cairns was responsible for probably the best shot against me when he clouted a perfectly good ball for six over square leg on a turning pitch at Hamilton. When he retired he had scored more sixes then anybody else in Test cricket; Viv Richards was in second place, to put that feat into perspective. With better luck on the injury front and better handling by certain coaches he would have been one of the real greats of the game. He had the style and sense to go out when he was ready instead of hanging on and declining in front of our eyes.

CHAPTER EIGHT

AUSTRALIA AND AUSTRALIANS

It has taken 15 years to complete the journey from promising youngster to senior player in the Australia side. Back in December 1991 when I was picked to play for Australia I was the second player of a start of a new generation. Mark Waugh had established himself with a brilliant debut hundred against England the year before. Then came players like Michael Slater, Matthew Hayden, Brendon Julian and Paul Reiffel. A year later Steve Waugh was recalled and a skinny kid from the New South Wales bush called Glenn McGrath followed after the 1993 Ashes. We were ready to push on together.

Remembering my first Australia team and looking at them now makes me feel quite old. David Boon and Merv Hughes are selectors, Allan Border has done that and moved on, Geoff Marsh has been and gone as Australia coach, Bruce Reid is our bowling coach at Hampshire, Ian Healy is president of the Players Association and Mark Taylor is on Cricket Australia's board of directors. The last pair are also television commentators. All of these guys I played with.

> For most of my career I've been lucky to play in a winning team. The ten years from 1995 will be remembered as one of the greatest passages in our history.

Then there is Greg 'Mo' Matthews, a quirky spin-bowling all-rounder who is playing grade cricket as competitively as ever at the age of 46. He is still a colleague of sorts – we both promote Advanced Hair Studio. 'Mo' gave me a lot of help in those early days and also came up with my first nickname as a Test player. He called me

'Mo' would be in my ear during games shouting: "Spin it up, Suicide!"

"Suicide" after the INXS song called 'Suicide Blonde' that we used to sing on the team bus. 'Mo' would be in my ear during games shouting: "Spin it up, Suicide!"

Now there are players around the squad who couldn't have been long out of shorts when I made my debut. As for Ricky Ponting, our captain, I can remember watching him in the nets at the Academy in Adelaide as a scrawny but highly talented 16-year-old. It gave me a real buzz when he led us for the first time. I have also presented Shane Watson and Nathan Hauritz with their one-day caps and Michael Clarke with his Test cap, in Bangalore. So I am one of the older guys now, and there are times when I feel it.

For most of my career I've been lucky to play in a winning team. The ten years from 1995 to 2005 will be remembered as one of the greatest passages in our history – that doesn't mean one of the greatest sides, just a very successful era. In one sequence we clocked up 16 Test wins in a row. So how did we do it? I guess that's the million dollar question, but there are no great secrets. Our domestic game produced good players, we gelled together, developed a winning habit, concentrated on doing the simple things well and never became complacent. Somewhere along the line we adopted a motto: when you are number one, prepare as though you are number two. Wise words indeed. Combined with some very talented players, some of the other countries in decline, and you have the result.

Our system from grade through to Pura Cup is universally recognised as the strongest in the world. At one point I reckon we could have picked at least two, maybe three teams from the Shield to take on any other country. We were leaving out batsmen like Darren Lehmann, Michael Bevan, Stuart Law and Jamie Cox when they scored stacks of runs at state level in Australia and for English counties as overseas players. Law smacked an unbeaten half-century on his Test debut and never played again; Martin Love made a hundred in his last Test.

You also have to look at the quality of the opposition. A lot of the best fast bowlers in the world were going out of the game around the turn of the decade – I can think of Waqar Younis, Wasim

Teams were losing their cutting edge and having to rebuild as we were going from strength to strength.

> The challenge over the next five years is to rebuild the team without losing our number one position. It will be interesting to see how the selectors decide to move forward.

Akram, Curtly Ambrose, Courtney Walsh and Allan Donald straight away. Teams were losing their cutting edge and having to rebuild as we were going from strength to strength. The final stage for us was the introduction of two of our most important players, Brett Lee and Adam Gilchrist.

Until then we did not have anybody with the sheer pace of Lee or a batsman as explosive as Gilchrist. He is more than handy coming in at number 7 because of his psychological impact on bowlers. Just as they think they have done the bulk of the work, he can knock them back again in half-an-hour. I remember a fantastic win against Pakistan at Hobart in 1999 when he put on 238 with Justin Langer after we were 126 for 5 chasing 369. That was a breakthrough game because we knew then that we could win any Test from any position. The opposition knew it too. Some teams turned up thinking they couldn't bowl to Hayden or Ponting or see off McGrath.

The challenge over the next five years is to rebuild the team without losing our number one position. It will be interesting to see how the selectors decide to move forward. I hope we learn from the past and change gradually. We cannot afford to lose four or five experienced players inside a year, but if we are not careful we could have the likes of Hayden, Langer, Martyn, Gilchrist, McGrath, MacGill, Gillespie and myself all leaving at roughly the same time. One or two of us might get a tap on the shoulder when we are not quite ready simply to smooth the transition. Having said that, each player is responsible for knowing when his time is up.

> I believe that senior players including myself have a responsibility to look at the bigger picture.

Unfortunately the increase in international cricket has meant the top batsmen and bowlers do not play as often in our domestic game. Youngsters are not therefore being exposed to the quality of cricket as consistently as previous generations. They take longer to come through and it must be a concern that players who have come in recently or are on the fringe such as Mike Hussey, Simon Katich, Andrew

Symonds and Brad Hodge are also in their 30s. I am a big believer in taking one or two young players on a tour to give them a taste of the international set-up. That way they are better equipped when the opportunity comes.

I believe that senior players including myself have a responsibility to look at the bigger picture. We have had a great time as Australia cricketers and we owe it to the next generation to be honest with ourselves and not hang around for too long.

We owe it to the next generation to be honest with ourselves and not hang around for too long.

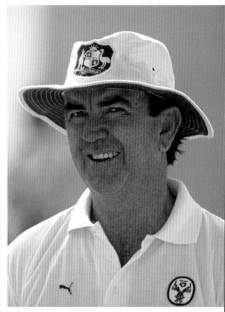

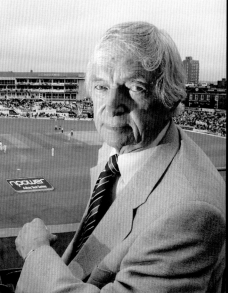

Allan Border was a legend in Australia cricket long before my Test debut. As well as regaining the Ashes he also led us to our first World Cup win in 1987 – he's being chaired by Dean Jones and Craig McDermott in this picture. AB gave me confidence in my early games by bringing me on to bowl when we needed wickets, not just as a stopgap. People forget how our game was at a low ebb when he took over. He played the percentages, played hard, stayed loyal and taught the next generation what it meant to play for Australia. He created an environment where we didn't accept losing.

Mark Taylor, here with a replica of the Ashes after winning the 1998-99 series, took more risks than Allan Border, but then he inherited a better team. He was probably the best captain I played under. He had a great cricket brain and was prepared to back his judgment even when it went against the grain. At one stage when the runs dried up, his captaincy probably helped to keep him in the side. But however down he felt inside, he always stayed positive around the team.

I was delighted when Ricky Ponting was appointed captain. Nothing against Adam Gilchrist, but I thought he had enough on his plate already. Keepers make ideal vice-captains because the position behind the stumps gives a great view of the game. There was never anything flash about 'Punter' – a nickname I gave him because he loves to bet on the greyhounds. He has stamped his own style on the job and his batting just gets better. Here, he is celebrating his hundred at Old Trafford in 2005.

previous pages
Steve Waugh goes out to bat for
Australia for the last time, on his home
ground at Sydney in 2004. I served as
vice-captain to Stephen for a while and
although we were chalk and cheese as
characters, we shared a mutual respect.
Like AB, he relished a fight and once he
grew into the job he helped to take
Australia to a new level. There were
some great players around him and
fantastic young talent coming through.
As a batsman I'd say he was a match-
saver rather than a match-winner.
When we were batting for time he
could play the way he really wanted.

However many wickets I have at the
end of my Test career I know the figure
would be lower but for the hands of
Ian Healy. He was the best keeper in my
time as an Australia player and he kept
out another fine gloveman, my mate
Darren 'Chuck' Berry from Victoria.
The keys for 'Heals' were his good
positioning and very quick, soft hands.
His reflexes were lightning fast.
I particularly remember one stumping
at Edgbaston in 1993 when he took the
ball from wide outside off stump to
remove Graham Thorpe. In this picture
Graeme Hick is the unfortunate
batsman.

I know that Adam Gilchrist – pictured
in action against Sri Lanka in 2006 –
will not be offended when I place him
behind Ian Healy as a pure wicketkeeper. What you also get with 'Gilly' is
a batsman who averages more than 50
and changes games with the speed
of his run-scoring. I think that side of
his game means that his keeping is
sometimes underestimated. Although
he is quite tall for the position this gives
him a bit more reach for wider catches.

Bobby Simpson could be quite strong
in his opinions but as my first coach for
Australia I think of him the same way
I think of Allan Border, the captain at
the time. 'Simmo' gave it to you straight,
as he saw it. He was quite unusual for a
coach in that he bowled a bit of leg-spin
so he was able to give me some quite
specialist help when I came into the
side. He was the bloke who really got
me in to bowling around the wicket as
an attacking device. The tactic has
brought some of my best wickets since.

Geoff Marsh, working out here with
Steve Waugh, had already played
alongside some of the guys when
he took over as coach. By that time
we were well on the way to becoming
the best side in the world and Marsh
realised that he didn't need to
implement great changes. He was
the right man because he gave us that
continuity. Marsh was a good listener,
and sometimes that is more useful
than an earful of dubious technical
advice.

In the past, it may have seemed to those on the outside that I haven't always agreed with John Buchanan, our current coach. But to his credit, 'Buck' is full of innovative ideas. He is constantly looking at ways to improve, be it through a new programme on his computer or the thoughts of an ancient Chinese warrior. Fair's fair, some people respond to that fairly well. And he does always stress that the team can take or leave his ideas.

I first met Terry Jenner during an abridged stay at our then-newish Academy in Adelaide in 1990. We've worked together ever since, and been good for each other. In the early days he was one of those who made me realise that I had to knuckle down and make the odd sacrifice. As a former Australia leggie himself he is a great technician who can spot straight away when part of my action is not quite right. From his viewpoint, working with me means he is back involved with the game he loves.

I lost a good mate when David Hookes died after an assault outside a bar in St Kilda in early 2004. The outpouring of grief reminded us all of his popularity, first as a dashing, young batsman and later as a coach. We had a lot of chats when he was coach of Victoria, my state side, and the conversations would always finish with me being a bit wiser. He also had a love of life and his strong opinions made him perfect for TV and radio.

Richie Benaud is the wise old man of cricket. He is famous nowadays for his work on television but many years ago he was a fine leg-spinner – our leading wicket-taker before Dennis Lillee broke the record. What I like about Richie is his generosity. He will always find time for a chat and has been very complimentary towards me down the years, but he doesn't make a big song and dance about his advice. In some countries you feel that former players are treated as has-beens but in Australia we have great respect for anybody who has worn the baggy green cap.

Mark Waugh was the master of the one-liner. As we both liked a drink and a bet on the horses it was obvious that we'd hit it off together. He was the kind of stylish batsman I would pay to watch, and a genuine match-winner. The two best Australian batsmen in my time would be Ricky Ponting and Mark. He was also a great all-round fielder – this catch got rid of Mannava Prasad at Sydney in 2000. It's a shame he keeps having a pop at the current players in his newspaper column now that he's retired – he used to hate people doing the same to him.

This is a fitting picture of Mervyn Gregory Hughes – he's at the centre of the action and he's the biggest bloke in the shot. It was taken during the Boxing Day Test at Melbourne against West Indies in 1992. By that time people had started to appreciate him as a genuine international class bowler and not just a character. Every dressing room could use a character like Merv, even if there were times when his belching and farting became a bit overpowering. Since he retired we've done a few dinners together and his stories still make me laugh even though I've heard them times over.

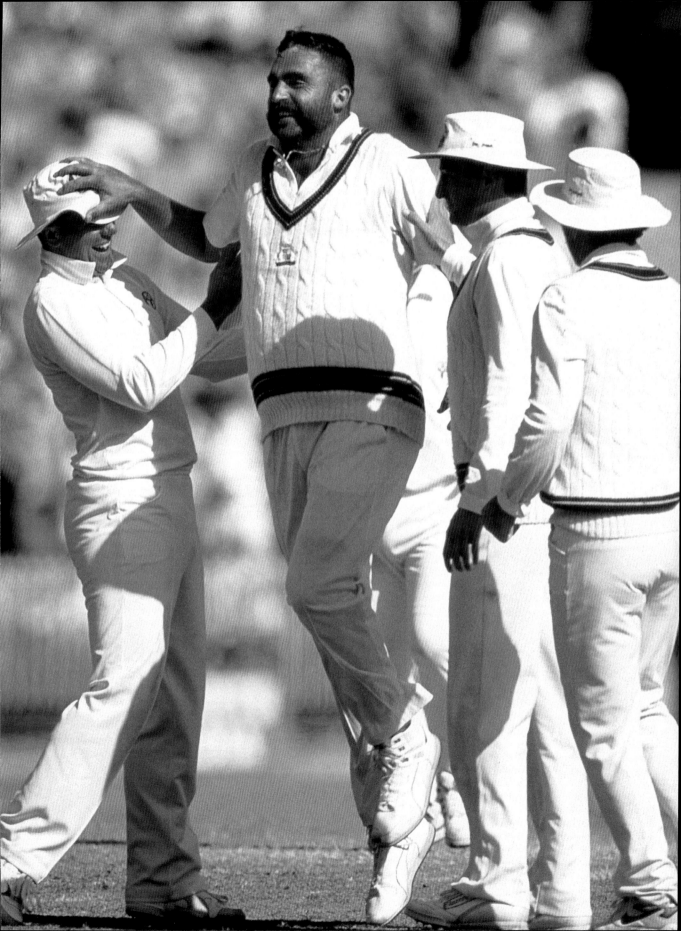

Darren Lehmann – or 'Boof' as we called him – was simply around at the wrong time. In another era he would have played 80 Tests and been recognised as one of the best players in the world. I was pleased he got a chance eventually and could show off his natural talent. In the one-day game he found gaps that other players couldn't see, let alone find. 'Boof' is a good mate, a loyal, laid-back guy with no pretensions who loves to chat about cricket over a beer and a fag, and never complains.

Glenn McGrath is one of the greats of the game and a model for any young pace bowler – he puts the ball in the right place consistently and does just enough with it. I always feel we can take wickets in tandem by creating pressure with dot balls. When he isn't on the field he can be a complete pest. When he gets bored he does things like hide your equipment or empty a sugar sachet over your head. On the field he gets what we call white-line fever and becomes this very angry, snarling bowler. Off it he's a lovely bloke who wouldn't hurt a fly.

Brett Lee has blossomed into one of the most dangerous bowlers in the world. With his raw pace he always had a good chance and now that he's had a run free of injuries he has established himself with the new ball. In this picture we're celebrating the wicket of Ian Bell at Edgbaston in 2005. When he came into the side I tried to help him with the odd word here and there so he could avoid some of the pitfalls away from the game. Maybe it should have been the other way around!

What I like most of all about Michael Clarke, to my right here at Hampshire, is his exciting brand of cricket. He is such a talented strokemaker, and off the field he can see the good in everything. I've taken him under my wing a little bit in the Australia team because he has such a big future. There are also times when he's helped me behind the scenes. In my opinion he is our best young batsman to emerge since Ricky Ponting, and a future captain.

CHAPTER NINE

ONE-DAY CRICKET

My first experience of watching professional cricket was a one-day game in Kerry Packer's World Series at VFL Park Waverley in Melbourne. It is a great format for the crowds and the beauty is that any side can beat another on a given day. Test cricket is different because over five days the better team always wins. Limited overs matches are less predictable. There are no draws and a tie means a great finish.

I don't remember much from my first game as a spectator: Australia against a World XI. But I do recall the uniforms, the sweeping flares and the sleeves that stopped before the bicep. Very flattering! Years later we had a running joke that nobody could play in the Australia one-day team if his waist size stretched beyond 38 inches. Mike Kasprowicz was the only guy I know who couldn't make it – he needed a 40. And Mark Taylor used to squeeze into 36s. Better a tight fit than admitting he needed 40s.

The limited overs game has changed so much since I started playing. In the early 90s the tactic was simple. If you were batting, just keep wickets in hand at all costs and then have a thrash in the final ten overs. A total of around 225 would be enough to win eight or nine games out of ten. Nowadays, unless the pitch is very bad, you would expect to lose 19 times out of 20 with that sort of score.

There have been so many innovations and matches it is easy to forget what the game was like even a dozen years ago. That is when we first had our names on the back of our shirts. There was a hilarious moment in our dressing room when somebody spotted Mike Whitney writing his name below the collar as if it were his school PE top. He didn't want anybody taking his shirt by accident. It hadn't registered that the word WHITNEY screamed from the back in huge capital letters.

As a bowler I try to split an innings into three phases. In the first 15 overs you are trying to take wickets. Batsmen want to attack and the best way to stop that is to remove them. From overs 16 to 40 the watchword is containment. This is where you need a good captain. You cannot just defend the boundaries because wise batsmen will work you around for five an over without any pressure and build a platform for the last ten. Ricky Ponting and Damien Martyn are masters. I like to have fielders up to make the batsman hit over the top for his runs. A couple of things to think about as a bowler: if you aim to go for 45 or fewer runs of your ten overs, that means you would be chasing 225; now if that's your final target, you're not losing too many. (5 x 45); on the subcontinent, say 50 for a total of 250.

> In the early 90s the tactic was simple. If you were batting, just keep wickets in hand at all costs and then have a thrash in the final ten overs.

The way batsmen run between the wickets is amazing now. You don't often see, for example, players amble a lazy single with a flick towards long leg. Running the first quickly puts pressure on a fielder and a slow reaction or a fumble can result in a second. Jonty Rhodes was the best in the world at that. He used to get runs that didn't look possible – you could add a few runs to his average because of those he earned for his partner. Mike Hussey today is another batsman who runs very well.

The final stage from the 41st to the 50th over is more scientific than ever. I think a good strategy is to bowl to a new batsman as you would normally – put in a slip, aim for the top of off stump with the odd short one and try to get him out. For a batsman who is settled, go for slower balls, yorkers and odd bumper. The trick is to keep him guessing with subtle variations. Ian Harvey was good at this – if anything he tried too many slower balls when he played for Australia. He used to practise yorkers and made himself into a very effective player

> This is where you need a good captain. You cannot just defend the boundaries because wise batsmen will work you around for five an over without any pressure and build a platform for the last ten.

– he was by far the best at executing the yorker. Batsmen can try to counter this by standing out of the crease to upset length, or stepping away to get into a position to manoeuvre the ball into gaps. The beauty of one-day cricket, 20 and 50 overs, is that it can appeal to everybody. Anybody coming new to the game can see the big hits, the quick runs, and soak up the atmosphere. Traditionalists have all that, but can also savour the mind games between batsman and bowler.

People who criticise the one-day game should reflect on how skills have passed into the Test arena. It has re-invigorated the five-day game.

People who criticise the one-day game should reflect on how skills have passed into the Test arena. It has re-invigorated the five-day game. Ground fielding is far better and you now see amazing sliding fielding and players throwing themselves around. Slower balls are now a weapon in the armoury of all the best pacemen in Tests. Batsmen have had to take on the best bowlers in 50 over matches and have drawn confidence from the results so they are now more adventurous when they go back to the first-class game. I think I am still pretty economical, but I don't think I would be allowed to return some of the really tight figures from my early days.

Sri Lanka made a big contribution with their approach in the 1996 World Cup, when Sanath Jayasuriya and Romesh Kaluwitharana began the innings with all guns blazing. That changed the thinking of other teams. We were all waiting for them to come a cropper but they went all the way to win the competition. 'Kalu' was an important figure in one-day cricket. He set the trend that Adam Gilchrist popularised. These days teams prefer a batsman/wicketkeeper to a wicketkeeper/batsman.

The way the game has gone was well illustrated when we played South Africa at the Wanderers in 2006. Talk about a crazy day. We scored 434, the highest total in a one-day international. Jacque Kallis apparently said that Australia were 15 runs short, but we still lost with a ball to spare. Batsmen went for their shots from the start and didn't let up all afternoon. Some of the bowling lacked imagination and might not have been great but everything was in favour of the batsmen – a short boundary, a good pitch and quick outfield – but they demonstrated what is possible with a bit of courage and ambition. I'm not sure that scores around 300 will ever become the norm, but I do think totals in general will keep getting bigger.

One argument that will probably never go away is about 'specialist' one-day players. In an ideal world I think the Test and one-day teams would be the same, but in reality that is hard to imagine. Even at a simple level, our success as a Test side was based on an attack with four bowlers – that would leave you ten overs short in one-day cricket straight away. In the opening positions you are not looking simply to see off the new ball. You want to take advantage of the fielding positions, demanding a different approach.

Michael Bevan was a very good one-day batsman, but did not enjoy the same success in Test cricket. He found a niche as a finisher who went in around the number six position with the task of being there at the end of the innings. If he was, then we almost always won. Bevan had the gift of being able to time a run chase almost to the last ball, sizing up each bowler and working out precisely where and when the runs would come. The team with the aggressive attitude was perfect to allow Bevo to bat this way.

> In an ideal world I think the Test and one-day teams would be the same, but in reality that is hard to imagine.

As for my own contribution, I like to think I helped to change attitudes towards spin bowling away from spearing the ball flat and defensively towards leg stump. In the old days some captains couldn't wait for the spinner to get through his ten overs in mid-innings and almost wiped his forehead in relief if he came through unscathed. Now, you might see a spinner inside the first 15 overs if the seamers have been smashed or even at the end to make batsmen put the pace on the ball.

In Australia in particular, the spinner can be very effective at the end of an innings because the grounds are bigger. It is a bit harder in places like the West Indies, South Africa and India where a miss-hit-hit can go ten rows back if the batsman has followed through. These shots look great on television but as a bowler you feel the game is just unfair. One-day cricket has certainly been designed for batsmen!

I think the rule about bouncers ought to be removed. If the ball goes over head height, then of course that is a wide. But the batters should be tested against the short ball and I don't think crowds would mind because the hook is one of the most spectacular shots in the book. I also think that the batting side should be able to call a five-over period where fielding restrictions apply and that one bowler should be allowed 12 overs in an innings instead of the usual ten.

In all, I played 194 one-day internationals, took 293 wickets and missed about 75 games through injuries and suspension. I played in two World Cup finals and was named Man of the Match when we won at Lord's in 1999. I am happy with my lot in one-day cricket. Did I pack it in too soon? Well, the farewell was not exactly as I hoped. My aim in the 2003 World Cup was to help Australia to retain the trophy. We won, but unfortunately I left before the first game to begin my enforced lay-off.

> # In all, I played 194 one-day internationals, took 293 wickets and missed about 75 games through injuries and suspension.

Since deciding to concentrate on Test cricket I feel I have bowled better than ever. The statistics back that up. So I do not regret my decision at all. One-day cricket is for young men. That's not to say I don't miss it. It is not just the games, which are intensive enough, but the three weeks or so at the end of a tour – or even longer in an Australia season – when you are living out of a suitcase playing in a different city every third day. Also the training to prepare for one-day cricket and all that throwing puts enormous pressure on my shoulder.

I thought that those weeks would be better spent with my family and children. I meant the decision to be final. I even handed down the number 23 to Michael "Pup" Clarke. This was a tradition I started, where a senior player hands down his shirt on retirement to a player who shares his belief in the way the game should be played. I gave mine to Michael Clarke.

> # I am 99.9 percent certain there will be no comeback. And I really hope the remaining 0.1 percent doesn't fuel more speculation.

By the way, I want to put on record how I became number 23 in the first place. There is a story that NIKE insisted I should have the same number as Michael Jordan, their great basketball player, as a marketing ploy. Rubbish! The fact is I was given 23 as an Aussie Rules player with St Kilda in 1987 – years before NIKE had ever heard of Shane Warne. Then when I was old enough to bet in a casino I began to go for the same number on the roulette wheel. I had a bit of luck with 23 red, and it stayed with me. I also liked the way Dermott Brereton played AFL Football: he was 23. My other favourite players were Peter Knights and the late Trevor Barker.

The story about a possible return for the 2007 World Cup does not seem to go away. I will try to nail it once and for all. I am 99.9 percent certain there will be no comeback. And I really hope the remaining 0.1 percent doesn't fuel more speculation. What I mean is this: if every other credible spinner in Australia has broken down and if Ricky Ponting says, "We need you mate, and there's nobody else", then I would have to consider it.

Bear in mind I will be 37 going on 38. I only play one-day cricket for Victoria these days when they lose players to Australia and have injuries or Cam White is away, so I captain. Speculation is unfair on Brad Hogg, who is doing a pretty good job for Australia. He also bats and fields well. There is no need for me to play. The selectors have been planning without me and I don't intend to disrupt those preparations. All being well, I will be cheering on Ricky, Brad, Michael Clarke as number 23 and a mate, and the rest from the comfort of my own sofa, or from a boat if someone offers me an invitation.

All being well, I will be cheering on Ricky, Brad, Michael Clarke as number 23 and a mate, and the rest from the comfort of my own sofa, or from a boat if someone offers me an invitation.

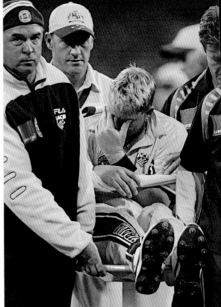

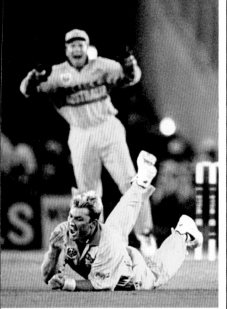

Mark Taylor described our World Cup semi-final against the West Indies in 1996 as the most unbelievable match of his career. Basically, they were cruising to the final with 43 needed from 45 balls and eight wickets in hand. I'd already managed to get Courtney Browne with a return catch and I still felt we had a chance. In a situation like that a new batsman is under immediate pressure, and under lights it is hard to pick up the pace straight away. So I knew that one wicket could change the tide. By the time I had Ian Bishop leg-before the initiative had swung.

There is no doubt about the lowpoint of my one-day career. We went into the 1996 World Cup final in Lahore as strong favourites to beat Sri Lanka but the truth is we were a bit flat most of the way through. Our preparation was not quite right. We were given bad information about the state of the ground after heavy rain, the lights were a bit iffy and we lost the toss. I was out stumped early after being pushed up the order as a pinch-hitter and then found the ball hard to grip because of the humidity. You can see the frustration as Arjuna Ranatunga turns for a run and then, at the end, as the Sri Lankans rush on to celebrate. Not long after I went in for a much-needed operation to repair my spinning finger.

I've never managed a hat-trick in a one-day international but I came close twice in this game against West Indies at Sydney in 1996. After bagging Roland Holder and Junior Murray I had a fantastic shout for leg-before here against Kenny Benjamin, only for the umpire to give him the benefit of the doubt. Then about 20 minutes later I managed to get Benjamin and Nixon McLean with successive balls – only for Courtney Walsh to get his bat down on a flipper.

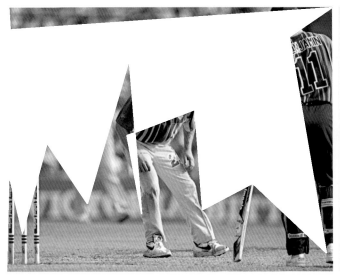

Nasser Hussain is well known for his fiery temper. That always made him vulnerable to a bit of chirp, as happened in this one-day game at Sydney in 1999. At the time, Nasser was trying to cement a regular place in the one-day side and fancied the idea of playing the hero. England just needed to keep the scoreboard ticking but I managed to wind him up so he went for big shots to try to make me look a mug. He was quickly stumped and England lost by 10 runs. Later on he became a good captain. He was not always everybody's cup of tea but he gave the side the right mindset and laid the foundations for Michael Vaughan.

I had plenty on my mind at the start of the 1999 World Cup in England. Simone was pregnant with our second child, Jackson, in Australia. Meanwhile my return from a shoulder operation was not going all that smoothly – I'd been dropped for the final Test against the West Indies before the tournament. That was a big knock, I wasn't sure where I stood and I was even thinking of retirement.

After a poor start to the World Cup we put ourselves in a situation where we were effectively playing six or seven finals – lose any one and our chances of lifting the trophy were gone. We brought in Tom Moody, gave Glenn McGrath the new ball, and our fortunes started to change – not least in this game against West Indies at Old Trafford. McGrath used the conditions brilliantly and the wicket here of Brian Lara was one of five for the big man. We could even manipulate the run rate in our innings to help us through to the next stage.

previous pages
Quite simply the greatest one-day game in history – nobody would disagree with my verdict of our 1999 World Cup semi-final against South Africa. I thought our score of 213 was a little short and Herschelle Gibbs was clearly out to make amends after dropping the World Cup – in the supposed words of Steve Waugh – at Headingley a few days earlier. When I came on to bowl I knew we needed something special. I just wanted to spin the ball as much as I could and I knew I was in business after ripping one past Gibbs to hit off stump. Not for the first time South Africa buckled under pressure, resulting in the famous run out between Allan Donald and Lance Klusener. The funny thing was, as we rushed towards the middle only a few of us knew the tie was good enough to take us into the final. I was named Man of the Match for my four wickets.

After our amazing games with South Africa I guess the 1999 World Cup final could be seen as an anti-climax. Pakistan can be erratic – brilliant one day, sloppy the next – and I think they were probably overawed by the occasion at Lord's. We learned from our mistakes three years earlier, made sure we kept everything nice and simple, avoided any distractions and won by eight wickets. It's easy to tell a guy to relax on a big occasion. There are bound to be nerves. But I've learned that what is good enough to get to a final is probably good enough to win it.

Within six weeks around Christmas and New Year 2002-03 I was twice carried off at the MCG. The emotions were rather different. First time, I needed the help of a stretcher after falling on my right shoulder. The pain was coursing through my body and with the World Cup less than two months away I feared the worst. Thanks to the great work of our medical team, however, I was back for the end of the VB Series and had the honour of being carried off after beating England in the final. That was due to be my last one-day international in Australia – unfortunately it proved to be my last anywhere. A drug test showed traces of a diuretic I'd taken purely for cosmetic reasons and brought a 12-month ban.

CHAPTER TEN

HAMPSHIRE

Hampshire has become an important part of my life in cricket. Southampton is now home, as I am a resident of the UK – I own a home and have based myself there. I feel as though I'm involved in a big adventure with the club. The sense that we are going places is due to the ambition of Rod Bransgrove, the chairman, and the players wanting to become the best they can and having ambitions of winning trophies, and the decision to move to a spanking new ground. It is a real honour to captain the side at one of the most exciting times in our history and I felt very proud when we won the Cheltenham & Gloucester Trophy in 2005.

My association with England actually goes right back to 1989 when I spent a season playing club cricket in Bristol. And I think because of the way the players and people of Bristol treated me, I have loved coming back; these were special times and some of the guys from those days have become close friends. I was back in England two years later, with Accrington in the Lancashire League. There were then offers from Northamptonshire in 1994 and a few others over the years, and Sussex in 1998. Both were attractive, but came at the wrong time. I first became aware that Hampshire might be interested when Robin Smith approached me via Ian Botham. The more I looked into the club, the more it felt right for me.

> I first became aware that Hampshire might be interested when Robin Smith approached me via Ian Botham.

Unfortunately things didn't work out straight away. I felt really sorry for Robin Smith, our captain. Luck does play a part and we were on the wrong end of a few situations we could do nothing about. For one, the summer did not help. I remember it rained the morning I arrived at the old Northlands Road ground and it was a good job I decided not to throw the umbrella away after that soggy morning.

Robin had retired by the time I returned in 2004, this time as captain. We were runners-up for the D2 title and managed to gain promotion in the Championship and finished third in the National League first division. Cricket produces reams of statistics, but the two columns that matter to me are the W and L columns. As a captain I'll always try to create a winning situation, even if a declaration opens the possibility of defeat. That's how you improve. You win some and lose some, but I will back my players to come through more often than not. Counties have a responsibility to produce England cricketers. It is good for youngsters to play under the pressure of trying to win at all times. This constant winning mentality can only improve players..

We had very talented players and I thought we were on the verge of becoming a real force, so it didn't surprise me to finish within three points of winning the Championship in 2005. We ended the season beating the champions, Nottinghamshire, by an innings and 188 runs. By scoring 714 for 5 – the best score by any county all season and a Hampshire record – we proved that Rose Bowl pitches are no longer a graveyard for batsmen. Although I think Nottinghamshire in that game didn't get much sleep after celebrating their championship win, and rightly so. The stadium is first-class and the facilities for players are excellent. Having played all over the world I can guarantee that the ground is ready to host Test cricket.

That season I achieved one of my ambitions by scoring a first-class hundred. It came against Kent at Canterbury with our last man, Richard Logan, at the crease. The crowd found it funny when I jumped up and punched the air in delight. Like all bowlers I enjoy trying to hit the ball as far as I can. I suffer enough punishment with the ball, so I try to dish some out as well. In England a lot of bowlers who can bat a bit are described as all-rounders and with another hundred against Middlesex a few weeks later I wonder whether I now qualify. (Ha Ha).

The debate about overseas players in county cricket has been going on for years. To my mind having the best players in the world in your domestic competition only raises the standard. My way of thinking is you should have eight players who are qualified to play for England and the three others can be made up of Cold Pak Overseas or someone from the Moon. How can it harm a young English batsman to face Shoaib Akhtar, Glenn McGrath or Muttiah Muralitharan? Anything that bridges the gap between county and international cricket is

Over the past decade Australians have given good service. That is reflected in the number of us now playing in England. I think the whole package has a lot to offer.

worthwhile. With 18 first-class counties there are still plenty of openings for English players. The best will always come through.

Clubs should do their homework and check character when they recruit. I believe an overseas player should offer something more than runs, wickets and catches. He is there to set an example in the way he goes about the game and find time to help emerging players on the staff. Over the past decade Australians have given good service. That is reflected in the number of us now playing in England. I think it has improved a lot of players who have gone there. The different conditions, the responsibility of being overseas, the expectations – I think the whole package has a lot to offer. Also developing life skills in socialising with the club and sponsors. If you put everything you have into trying to improve as a player and improving the English county players, then it can be a very enjoyable and rewarding time in your life.

Having said that, it can be a tough job. In truth there probably are too many games during the season. Six months is a long time when you are playing day-in, day-out. There is not long enough to work on skills, prepare, or sit back and really analyse something that is going wrong. The positive side is to experience so many different pitches and conditions in a short time. It annoys me to hear people knock the county game. If it produces a guy like Andrew Flintoff, I'd suggest it can't be too bad. Overall, there are only a few things I would change: I would scrap the bonus points system. I know with rain, etc. some teams have more chance of missing games but, hey, imagination from captains can set up a game. Ideally, I'd have points for first innings and points for winning. This would stop teams trying to get maximum batting and bowling points by manipulating the current system. As things stand at the moment, it is possible for substandard teams to win the championship purely by winning the odd game. As Warwickshire actually did, winning only five games. All one-day competitions except Twenty20 should be 50 overs because that's what the next level is, not 40.

Having been to England a number of
times before I wasn't really surprised
to find the rain pouring down when
I arrived at Hampshire in April 2000.
What took me back was the way it
continued for a large part of the season.
There was a lot of publicity about my
arrival. In general batsmen were
reluctant to take many risks and
I seemed to get away with the odd
bad ball on my reputation – they were
looking for traps that just weren't there.

Robin Smith was my first Hampshire
captain and one of the reasons I joined
the county. At an early press conference
I think he mentioned that I like to enjoy
myself off the field, which amazed me
because 'the Judge' was probably the
most sociable bloke in cricket. He was a
good man to lead Hampshire because
he cared deeply about the county and
he felt he'd let people down when we
were relegated from the Championship.
That was rubbish. Nobody tried harder
than Robin Smith.

My first season at Hampshire was our last at Northlands Road. It was very cosy and had a lot of character but after 115 years the time had come to move on. Even though people felt emotional at the time, you only have to look around the new Rose Bowl to realise the club made the right decision. One feature I remember about Northlands Road was the big, old bell (below) to the left of the pavilion.

At the start of every season there is a Media Day where we pose for photographs and answer questions from the press. These pictures were taken in 2004 when I began my second spell. The start of a season in England and Australia is always a time of great optimism – you're back on level terms with every other side and feel ready to take on the world. We had a new song called 'Glory, glory, we are Hampshire' and we screeched it out a few times as we won promotion in the Championship.

I played alongside Kevin Pietersen for
the first part of the 2005 season but
this was our first of many encounters as
opponents. Hampshire took on England
in a one-day warm-up at the Rose Bowl
a couple of days before the Twenty20
international, a great day for all those
who put so much time and effort in
getting the stadium up and running.
I hope it isn't too long before Pietersen
is playing in a Test match here because
the facilities for players are probably
second only to Lord's in England.

Three days after the Ashes I was back playing for Hampshire against Glamorgan. I won't forget the drive to Cardiff in a hurry. Every time I came to a stop another driver seemed to wind down his window and shout 2-1, 2-1. Thanks – I'd forgotten the scoreline. I can understand why England wanted to rest their players after such a draining few weeks, but we could have used Pietersen for the climax. I think a lot of those guys would love to have helped their counties at a crucial time.

I really enjoy captaining the side and it's unfortunate that I have never been able to lead Australia in a Test match. Hampshire put me in charge in 2004 and I like to think I've instilled some good habits in the side. There is always a lot to think about on the field – this picture was taken in 2005 and it looks as though I'm directing traffic rather than setting a field. I guess my philosophy comes down to this: I want players to take responsibility for their own game and always, always play for the team.

As a captain you take a lot of pleasure when one of your guys is picked for his country. Usually it happens to a youngster such as Chris Tremlett, who made his one-day international debut for England in 2005 and would have played in the final Test at the Oval if the selectors had shown more faith. But even experienced players can put themselves in the frame – as Shaun Udal proved when he won his first cap at 36. I helped him develop a 'slider' – a ball that goes straight on – and it was to his great credit that he worked to get it right at an age when others are thinking about retirement.

CAREER STATISTICS

Test debut: Australia v India at Sydney – Jan 2-6, 1992
Last Test: South Africa v Australia at Johannesburg – March 31-April 4, 2006
ODI debut: New Zealand v Australia at Wellington – March 24, 1993
Last ODI: Asia XI v ICC World XI at Melbourne – Jan 10, 2005
First-class span: 1990/91 - 2005/06
List A span: 1991/92 - 2005/6
Twenty20 span: 2004-2005

PERSONAL BESTS

ENGLAND
90, Old Trafford 2005 & 8-71, Brisbane 1994-95

INDIA
86, Adelaide 1999-2000 & 6-125, Chennai 2004-05

NEW ZEALAND
99, Perth 2001-02 & 6-31, Hobart 1993-94

PAKISTAN
86, Brisbane 1999-2000 & 7-23, Brisbane 1995-96

SOUTH AFRICA
63, Cape Town 2001-02 & 7-56, Sydney 1993-94

SRI LANKA
35, Colombo 1992 & 5-43, Galle 2003-04

WEST INDIES
47, Brisbane 2005-06 & 7-52, Melbourne 1992-93

ZIMBABWE
6, Harare 1999-2000 & 3-68, Harare 1999-2000

Wisden Cricketer of the Year 1994

Selected as one of five *Wisden* Cricketers of the
Century 2000

Statistics compiled at the time of Australia's 3-0 win
over South Africa at the beginning of April 2006.

BATTING AND FIELDING AVERAGES

CLASS	MAT	INNS	NO	RUNS	HS	AVE	BF	SR	100	50	4s	6s	CT	ST
TESTS	138	192	16	2947	99	16.74	5152	57.20	0	11	330	35	119	0
ODIs	194	107	29	1018	55	13.05	1413	72.04	0	1	60	13	80	0
FIRST-CLASS	263	360	42	5960	107	18.74			2	22			222	0
LIST A	285	179	35	1722	55	11.95			0	1			114	0
TWENTY20	2	2	0	12	12	6.00	14	85.71	0	0			0	0

BOWLING AVERAGES

CLASS	MAT	BALLS	RUNS	WKTS	BBI	BBM	AVE	ECON	SR	4	5	10
TESTS	138	38733	16997	674	8/71	12/128	25.21	2.63	57.46	45	35	10
ODIS	194	10642	7541	293	5/33	5/33	25.73	4.25	36.32	12	1	0
FIRST-CLASS	263	66268	29984	1167	8/71		25.69	2.71	56.78		57	11
LIST A	285	15244	10761	429	5/33	5/33	25.08	4.23	35.53	18	2	0
TWENTY 20	2	48	51	1	1/29	1/29	51.00	6.37	48.00	0	0	0

INDEX

Information in captions is indexed as text
Page numbers in *italics* refer to illustrations

PHOTOGRAPHY CREDITS

ACKNOWLEDGEMENTS

To Brooke, Jackson and Summer – you guys are my inspiration and my life, I love being your Dad and I love the way you put a smile on my face and make me feel amazingly happy. Love you guys. This is my Agent, Michael Cohen and me at Lord's unveiling my portrait; he is a very good friend and a wonderful Manager, thank you, Michael. To my Mum and Dad, Keith & Brigitte, thank you for all your support and friendship and being such unbelievable and great parents and being fantastic grandparents to Simone and my children, we all love you very much. To Jas, what can I say, mate! Without our sledging, competitive games of tennis, cricket, football – you name it, we did it together – thank you also for being my manager, agent, friend, brother and just being there and being you – love you, mate.

THE SHANE WARNE
F O U N D A T I O N
teaming up to help aussie kids

Text: Shane Warne with Richard Hobson
Art Director: Auberon Hedgecoe
Design: Ashley Western
Editor: Karen Dolan
Picture Research: Jennifer Veall
Statistics: Richard Hobson and www.baggygreen.com.au
Index: Dorothy Frame

First published in Great Britain in 2006 by Cassell Illustrated, a division of Octopus Publishing Limited, 2-4 Heron Quays, London E14 4JP

A CIP catalogue record for this book is available from the British Library.

ISBN-13: 9781844035434
ISBN-10: 1-84403-543-3

10 9 8 7 6 5 4 3 2

Printed by Loce, Italy